Saint Nicholas

Bishop of Myra

Saint Nicholas

Bishop of Myra

The Life and Times of the Original Father Christmas

D.L. Cann

NOVALIS

Cover design: Caroline Gagnon
Cover illustration: Anne Côté
Layout: Caroline Gagnon, Suzanne Latourelle

Business Office:
Novalis
49 Front Street East, 2nd Floor
Toronto, Ontario, Canada
M5E 1B3

Phone: 1-800-387-7164 or (416) 363-3303
Fax: 1-800-204-4140 or (416) 363-9409
E-mail: cservice@novalis.ca
www.novalis.ca

National Library of Canada Cataloguing in Publication

Cann, David L
Saint Nicholas, Bishop of Myra : the life and times of the original Father Christmas / David L. Cann.

Includes bibliographical references and index.
ISBN 2-89507-308-2

1. Nicholas, Saint, Bishop of Myra. 2. Christian saints—Turkey—Myra (Ancient city)—Biography. I. Title.

BR1720.N46C36 2002 270'.092C2002-903744-1

Printed in Canada.

We acknowledge the financial support of the Government of Canada through the Book Publishing Industry Development Program (BPIDP) for our publishing activities.

10 9 8 7 6 5 4 3 2 1 10 09 08 07 06 05 04 03 02

Contents

Acknowledgments

My thanks begin with my wife, Karen, who has supported this adventure with enthusiasm and great endurance for ten years. A trek across southwest Turkey in the month of August is not for the faint of heart.

My deepest gratitude and heartfelt appreciation I extend to Kevin Burns, Michael O'Hearn, Anne Louise Mahoney, Jennifer Rae-Brown and the consummate professionals at Novalis for their vision and support of this project.

I am also grateful to my friends in the Orthodox Church, who provided support and critical review while I composed the manuscript. Among these friends in Christ, I thank especially Father Pierre Vachón (a veteran monk of Mount Athos, Greece, and a fearless French Canadian ice-hockey player), the Right Reverend Bishop Seraphim, the Reverend Doctor Symeon Rodger, the Very Reverend Ghattas Hajal, Leslie Brigid Still, the Very Reverend Daniel Matheson and Dougald Gander.

Preface

Sometimes it is the naive questions that open the greatest vistas for us. This project evolved from a desire to discover the original Saint Nicholas of Myra. The effort to make that discovery took me to some of the dustiest corners on earth—the coastal mountains and rugged seaside valleys of southwest Turkey, and the shelves of Graeco-Roman history in university libraries. On that journey of discovery, I learned a few unexpected lessons. Not the least valuable of those lessons is that one can relieve hyperthermia by drinking hot, black tea. The greatest lesson is that Saint Nicholas of Myra is a real person in history who lived a courageous and inspirational life.

It is an unexpected gift that Saint Nicholas of Myra emerges as a heroic and holy person—one whose life has much to give in our present era. It seems ironic and unfair that the saint whom countless people in the past and present have called upon to protect them from injustice has himself been misrepresented in history. Therefore, let us take a journey of discovery together—through the rugged lands and over the restless seas that were once part of the Roman Empire, and across the ages from the fourth century CE to the present—to find the original Saint Nicholas.

Introduction

My first memories of Saint Nicholas are from when I was a child living in a coastal town along the North Atlantic Ocean. I learned that Saint Nicholas was a magical, white-bearded gentleman who brought gifts at Christmastide to all children everywhere. Naturally I was enthralled and intensely curious about such a wonderful person. I can remember reading every scrap of Saint Nicholas lore I could lay my hands on, and I sat up at night to gaze out my window on Christmas Eve for some sign of his arrival. After many Christmas seasons passed and I failed to encounter Saint Nicholas, the immediacy of my childhood fascination with him faded. I held to my hope, however, that I would encounter Saint Nicholas one day.

Thus began my lifelong search for the illumined ones in history, those who have gone before us whom we know as saints, and especially for Saint Nicholas of Myra. Saint Nicholas is one of the saints whose popularity has been based upon few facts and much legend. In my search for historical truth about Saint Nicholas I have travelled from Athens, Greece, to Myra (Kale), Turkey, from research libraries in Western Europe and North America to chapels, churches and museums in the Eastern Mediterranean. The more knowledge I gained of the historical Saint Nicholas, the more I came to see how his devoted followers from both West and East have transformed him in legend. It became clear that the patina of the Saint Nicholas legend offers more insight about his followers than it does about him. The colour and texture with which diverse cultures have painted Saint Nicholas in legend illuminates both their depth of reverence for sainthood and their need to seek the divine—to feel the grace, love and protection of God.

Like so many devoted followers of Saint Nicholas, I too have felt drawn by both a reverence for sainthood and a personal need to seek the divine. In searching, I have come to see that a saint is a most tangible icon of holiness, and Saint Nicholas is a most colourful emissary of divinely inspired generosity to the world.

My journey of discovery began as a fascination born of childish naïveté and my reluctance to give up Father Christmas. The question of whether there is a Father Christmas becomes less naive when we consider his origin in the real person, Saint Nicholas. When we search the Greek tradition, both saint literature and history offer clues to the events of his life. Facts of Graeco-Roman history in the fourth century CE and first-hand visits to ancient sites in Asia Minor (now Turkey) provide evidence that Saint Nicholas lived, and that certain historical events and places influenced him. What emerges from our search into the true story of Saint Nicholas of Myra is that he lived a heroic and holy life at a revolutionary moment in history.

What compels us to seek the factual story of Saint Nicholas is that his true identity as a person in history brings far richer meaning and inspiration than does the figure of Father Christmas who represents him today. Other works present the story of how Western Europeans fashioned Saint Nicholas into Father Christmas. This narrative takes us on an Eastern adventure in which we search far into ages past, learn what we can about Nicholas, Bishop of Myra, on the Mediterranean coast of Asia Minor during the dramatic fourth century, and discover the *true* Saint Nicholas!

The story of Saint Nicholas begins in a place and time of epic grandeur—the Eastern Roman Empire during the late third century. In that time, the Roman Empire extended from Britain, Gaul, Spain, Italy and Africa in the west to the Balkans, Greece, Asia Minor, Egypt and Palestine in the east. The Empire's territory spanned a distance of about 4,000 kilometres from west to east and about 2,000 kilometres from north to south, and it surrounded the Mediterranean Sea. The Romans interconnected the marvellous cities of their provinces with hundreds of paved roads and a system of post stations for travel by horse. Yet the Mediterranean Sea was the circulatory system of the Empire. Upon its navigable courses merchant mariners conveyed a huge volume of goods, people and culture.

Those who travelled the azure seaways of the Mediterranean spread Christian culture, saint stories and tales about Saint Nicholas. Gospel stories about Christ's birth and baptism, and popular saint stories from the Christian Greek spoken tradition flourished along with Eastern Roman civilization. Greek storytellers and Byzantine hagiographers, or writers of saint stories, have handed down to us the legends about Saint Nicholas of Myra. They tell us in grand and colourful passages of the beloved saint who braved one of the most catastrophic periods in the history of the Christian Church.

Saint Nicholas, as he comes to us in the Greek stories, is a person of great spiritual authority, that is, he has great wisdom and compassion, such as can be achieved only by those who live in complete and selfless dedication to God. Like other saints, Nicholas became famous because of miracles and wonders attributed to him, but his place among the saints does not depend on such stories. At Myra, Bishop Nicholas established his spiritual authority by his deeds. The true events of his life show him to have been a bishop who placed the needs of others ahead of his own, even when this meant sacrificing himself. By his acts of love and justice, Bishop Nicholas demonstrated the qualities we regard as essential to the spiritual authority of a saintly person. Saint Nicholas is among the revered company of saints who lived a heroic and holy life, independent of miracles or wonders.[1]

The poverty of facts and the wealth of fiction surrounding the life of Saint Nicholas make discovering his true story a challenge. Yet the available sources of information contain certain common elements that suggest a coherent sequence of events. Nicholas was born during the late third century in Patara, Lycia, in the region of Asia Minor. As a young man, he served as a Christian priest in Patara. Early in the fourth century, he moved 50 kilometres east to become Bishop of Myra, capital of the province of Lycia. Nicholas of Myra became famous for his faith, service and miracles. He made witness to his faith when he suffered during Emperor Diocletian's persecution of the Christians. Some Greek historians recorded that he attended the Council of Nicaea in the year 325. He died at Myra, and was ultimately buried in the small basilica that bears his name. During the tenth century, Prince Vladimir of Russia brought relics of Saint Nicholas from Constantinople (now Istanbul) to Kiev. In the eleventh century, Italian mariners transported Saint Nicholas' remains to Bari, Italy. These are all the historical facts available about Saint Nicholas.[2]

Since we have evidence that Saint Nicholas served as Bishop of Myra in Lycia during the fourth century, and since we have stories from the Greek spoken tradition recorded by Byzantine hagiographers, we can look to the primary sources from that period to learn what his life was like. In essence, we can be confident *that* he lived and we can infer *how* he lived.

From these moorings, we embark upon a turbulent sea of legends about the third most popular figure, after Jesus and his mother Mary, among Christians of both the West and the East. Our purpose is to discover from the texts of Saint Nicholas stories what truly can be attributed to him. We will analyze legends for their elemental facts and construct a reliable story from them. First, we will select only the legends from Greek hagiographic sources, carefully avoiding the fanciful accounts of Nicholas that originated in medieval Western Europe. Next, we will apply a textual analysis based upon the principle that the events of each legend must be simple and reasonable. Finally, we will fit the events of each legend with what we know of Nicholas and the setting in which he lived.[3]

We can accept the kernels of truth in the selected Nicholas stories for at least three reasons. Firstly, in almost every case where the cult of a saint has arisen, there has been conclusive evidence that a real person existed as its source—the memorial Church of Saint Nicholas at Myra is evidential in this regard. Secondly, while the storytelling around saints displays certain conventions of style, such as the didactic use of the number three to illustrate the Holy Trinity, the essential events of the stories are unique to the saint—for example, we know Nicholas and no other saint as the Bishop of Myra during the early fourth century. Thirdly, when we contrast the stories with first-hand historical sources, we find consistency—Lactantius and Eusebius, who were fourth-century historians, describe names and events that we find in stories about Saint Nicholas of Myra.[4]

With effort, we identify a handful of Saint Nicholas stories that ring true. For the setting, we look to the writings of Eusebius and Lactantius, both eyewitness historians of the reigns of Diocletian and Constantine. We also consult other reliable histories of third- and fourth-century Rome. We refer to a modern travel journal that records my journey from Greece and across the Aegean Sea to a stay in Myra, Turkey, to experience the culture and setting of Nicholas' environs. The journal records the sense of time and place that we use in order to visualize the world of Saint Nicholas, as described in this excerpt:

> It was getting late in the afternoon, so while daylight remained we drove to Kale [Myra] to find the original Church of Saint Nicholas. After some searching around Kale, we found the site about two blocks west of the town centrum. As at the earlier site, we paid a small admission fee. The entrance led us down a stone ramp into an excavated area, where we found ourselves looking into the south entrance of the restored ancient Byzantine church.
>
> At last, the Church of Saint Nicholas! This was where the legendary Nicholas had been honoured by the building of this church in which he had

been entombed. Near this church is possibly where Nicholas guided a community of Christians through the terrible years of persecution issued by the Augustus Emperor Diocletian during the early fourth century.

We stepped slowly inside. The church was constructed of stone, and followed the general plan of a basilica. Yet, it strayed somewhat from this design. A careful look around revealed that this house of worship was in fact a composite of construction from a few different periods. The central narthex was in the basilica, the largest and most recent part of the building perhaps dating to the sixth century. The north side of the church appeared to be older and was barely free of the alluvial earth that had once held the whole building.

The features of this Byzantine shrine were extraordinary. Domed chapels ringed the narthex. Stone niches built into the walls housed ornate marble sarcophagi, one of which was that of Saint Nicholas. The floors were decorated with elaborate tile mosaics. The doors and windows arched towards cement-surfaced, domed ceilings upon which we could see dimly the painted images of prophets and saints.

From the west entrance, into the narthex of the Church of Saint Nicholas streamed the rose and gold rays of the setting sun. They cast an amber light upon the apsis and synthronon, illuminating the six columns that stood about the altar so they appeared to glow like lamps.

In composing the life of Saint Nicholas we come upon episodes where reliable information simply has not been available; in such cases we are obliged to carefully reconstruct missing parts of his life based on informed conjecture. This said, we constantly observe the condition that any assumptions we make are in line with the facts that we do know. We are now prepared to construct a narrative that respects the truth of Nicholas' life and times.

From the sources described above, we will form our characterization of Saint Nicholas. He loved God foremost and loved dearly his fellow sojourners on earth. He took up the vocation of priest to help nourish the souls and lives of his beloved sisters and brothers. He provided gifts of support to those in need, thereby contributing to the survival and renewal of families within the community. As bishop, Saint Nicholas understood the nature of evil and struggled valiantly against it, courageously putting himself at risk during the Great Persecution in order to protect others. He paid a hard price in his struggle, suffering in captivity for years. After his release, he worked selflessly to rebuild the community of faithful in Myra, and to return to the vocation he loved best—worshipping God and ministering to his beloved parish.

Ironically, the modern view of Saint Nicholas as merely a white-bearded, grandfatherly man who passes out gifts at Christmastide is far too limited. We shall come to know the true Saint Nicholas to have been a guardian of souls, a protector of children and families, and an advocate for justice, as well as a giver of gifts.

In the chapters that follow, we will journey with Nicholas through his life, from his childhood in Patara to his preparation for and service as a priest in that town and, ultimately, to his heroic years as Bishop of Myra. Along the way, we will learn about the setting by two unique methods: on the one hand, by listening to the descriptions of places and events by eyewitnesses and informed commentators and, on the other, by transporting ourselves by way of visualizations in which we experience a place or event as though we were present at that moment in history.

Historians and tellers of saint stories offer us few details about the life of Nicholas. We have, however, a wealth of observations about the fourth-century culture and setting of the Eastern Roman Empire. Therefore, let us discover the true Saint Nicholas to the extent that historical narrative allows by walking the streets that he walked, meeting the people of the region, living the experiences of a resident of the era and sensing in every possible way the life and times of Saint Nicholas. We will conclude our journey by visiting the modern Christian descendants of the ancient Romans to see how they regard Saint Nicholas and how they celebrate Christmas.

Our search to encounter Saint Nicholas reaches before our time to our ancestors in ages and regions past. Our journey is at once a search for the historical Saint Nicholas and a search for the divine. We embark upon that search today, when our need for the divine and the hope it brings is as poignant for us in our time as it was for those who lived in ages before us.

Chapter I

Nicholas as a Youth in Patara

The story of Nicholas begins in Patara, a town on the Mediterranean coast of Asia Minor in the Roman province of Lycia, about the year 275. According to Greek tradition, Patara is where Nicholas was born and raised. It was here that cultural, philosophical and religious influences shaped Nicholas—first into a Christian youth, then a young priest and, ultimately, a bishop. In order to understand how Nicholas would have lived as a boy, let us explore the culture and environs of this town on the coast of what is now Turkey.

Patara was a minor town located in a region of major importance to the Roman Empire. The province of Lycia was part of Rome's treasure chest in the East. Lycia, like its neighbouring provinces in Asia Minor, served as both a breadbasket and military recruiting ground for Rome. In the countryside, agriculture flourished, while the cities bustled with people and industry. The populace consisted of Greek-speaking citizens, freed people and slaves, all of whom followed the same customs, beliefs and habits as their neighbours in Achaea (Greece).[5]

Patara, a small coastal town, enjoyed some sea trade but relied mostly upon cottage craft industry to support its approximately 15,000 people. Like other culturally Greek towns of its size, Patara shared in the imperial culture of the Roman Empire, but retained the Greek language and Hellenistic culture of the East. One mark of Hellenistic culture was the worship of the Olympian deities who, over the centuries, had become absorbed into the official pantheon of the Roman Empire.[6]

Gentle hills surrounded Patara, which lay in a valley about seven kilometres wide. Two entrances provided access to the town: a grand stone arch on the northern inland side and a notch in the southern hillsides to provide a way to the Mediterranean Sea.

Nicholas grew up here, in this modest but stylish coastal town. As he played, went to school and visited neighbours, Nicholas moved over streets that were paved with stone and lined with ornate temples, colourful shops and homes, as well as imperious public buildings decorated with columns and bas-reliefs. Nicholas meandered up the market streets passing shops that brimmed with colour and interest. Vendors filled their stands to overflowing with baskets, pots, barrels and amphorae packed with local varieties of grains, fish, fruits, vegetables, cheeses, herbs, oils and wines.

In the morning, the shops flourished at their best and busiest. A fresh and savoury breeze drifted in from the sea. The shopkeepers chatted with one another as they unfurled their brightly coloured awnings that rippled playfully above their heads. They set their baskets of goods out for display, carefully arranging the vegetables, fruits, nuts, grains and fish to appeal to the appetites of passing customers. The produce vendors and fishmongers arranged appetizing displays, and the bakers and spice vendors created tantalizing aromas. The smells of freshly baked breads and pastries mingled with the exotic scents of cinnamon, cardamom, basil and thyme.

Townspeople made their way to the market district seeking ingredients for the meals of the day. The shoppers dressed in full-length, long-sleeved tunics of linen and wool in colours ranging from white to red. Some wore straw hats and carried reed baskets. They scrutinized the day's produce and haggled with the vendors. The children wore little tunics that seemed to imitate those of the adults. Gazing up to their parents, the children followed closely their inspection of the goods on display in the stalls.

As Nicholas made his way to school, he might have stood in one of the avenues, or *plateia*, and looked towards the hilltops farther south. He would have seen the columned buildings of the acropolis, or high city. Any town of appreciable size had its acropolis, where one deity or another from the Graeco-Roman pantheon could be expected to watch over the town from a high temple. In times of danger, the acropolis provided a defensible refuge for the townspeople. At the acropolis in Patara, in keeping with the custom observed by pagans in most other Greek-speaking towns and cities, worshippers gave special honour to a female deity. In Athens, the reigning goddess was Athena, fabled giver of wisdom and champion of war, whose statue commanded the Acropolis from her temple, the Parthenon. In Ephesus, the goddess Artemis, the legendary huntress and moon goddess who watched over women, was the divine patroness. The Greeks at Ephesus built the temple of Artemis on a grand scale—the Artemisium at Ephesus covered four times the area of the Parthenon in Athens. As a humble Lycian neighbour to the southeast of the grand city of Ephesus, Patara was within the orbit of the goddess Artemis.[7]

The most striking architectural feature of Patara stood at the foot of the acropolis, built into the last hillside before the sea: the outdoor theatre, large enough to entertain most of the town's residents. Artisans used local, cut stone to build the theatre and create elegant arches and landings. With 25 tiers of seats encompassing a proscenium approximately 50 metres long, the theatre offered an impressive setting for performances. It was a popular venue for the citizens of Patara, a place where they could spend hours enjoying dramas, musical performances, dances, comedies and spectacles.

Patara resembled other Graeco-Roman settlements of its size. On the edge of town was a Jewish suburb with a synagogue. The main gates on the inland entrance to Patara outlined three arched portals made of cut stone; over these, two niches displayed statuettes of Olympian deities. The gates opened landward onto a verdant and rolling pastoral scene of pagan shrines, cemeteries, villas, farms, orchards and vineyards. Entering the northern gates and facing south, visitors moved seaward into the town. Patara had two or three main plateia that began at the town gates. Shops and houses built of masonry stood one to four stories high and lined the plateia. Some of the buildings offered the refreshing shade of roofed colonnades. Plateia converged at intersections in the town, creating open areas with market squares, called *agorae.*

Towns like Patara treated their agorae as decorative showcases, filling them with fountains, statues, bas-reliefs, mosaics and murals. The town councils decorated their agorae within the limits of their resources, and yet, even in a town the size of Patara, they probably endowed their public spaces with marble and bronze statuary portraying Greek gods and goddesses in various poses, colourful and dramatic portraiture of the Olympians in mosaic tile and brilliant paint on the pavements and walls, and leafy Corinthian ornamentation in bas-relief on the stone buildings. The most impressive of the ornate agorae supported the municipal council hall, magistrate's court, library, pagan temples and baths.

The agorae were also the sites of grammar-school classes. The pedagogue, usually hired by the city council, conducted classes in the open air on one of the porticoes that faced the intersection, or trivium, where three plateia met. The pedagogue taught young Nicholas and the other girls and boys of the city the basics of grammar, arithmetic and reading, and supplemented their lessons with selections from the Greek classics, which, of course, would have included Homer's *Iliad*. Nicholas and the other students dutifully practised their written lessons on slates with chalk, or on wooden tablets that contained writing surfaces filled with beeswax. Using the pointed end of a stylus, the students imprinted their Greek words and phrases into the surface of the beeswax and, when finished with each lesson, rubbed out the impressions on the wax using the blunted end of the stylus.

Fourth-century artisans made running water available in the agorae and other public places, as well as in the most privileged households. Bathing was therefore a public activity in the civic bathhouses. The public baths presented Christians with an ambiguous ethical situation. To take a bath among other people was not in itself a sinful thing for a Christian to do, but the bathhouses were, by common knowledge, places of occasional indiscreet behaviour. Christians who wished to remain beyond moral reproach probably opted to bathe in private, rather than at the bathhouse in the town agora.

Despite the hedonistic features of the agorae, bathhouses and theatre, Patara offered its Christian residents more rural virtues than urban vices. The poorer people who worked in trades and crafts in and around the mercantile districts of Patara lived by the values of the countryside. Industry in Patara was probably at the cottage craft level—labour-intensive goods and services primarily for local use and consumption—with at least some trade with regional centres such as Ephesus, Rhodes and Myra. Patarans worked in food-processing, textiles, pottery, woodworking, glass, metalworking, leather, bone and shell crafts, brick and tile, and stoneworking. Food processors milled grains and baked breads and pastries, caught fish and preserved them, picked olives and pressed olive oil, grew and harvested fruits, vegetables and nuts, and cultivated grapes and pressed wine. Textile workers prepared, spun, wove and dyed wool, cotton, flax and other fibres to produce cloth.

Potters in a town the size of Patara concentrated on work for local customers who needed coarse products for their homes, that is, serving ware, lamps and storage containers. Woodworkers produced fine works that included tools, furniture and carvings. Glass-workers had learned the glass-blowing art, probably from Syrians, and produced, decorated and coloured vessels of blown glass as well as formed pieces. Leather, bone and shell crafters made a variety of useful and decorative items for personal use: leather gear for pack animals, clothing and containers, and bone and shell for combs, jewellery and implements. Metalworkers produced much of their fine work in gold, silver and bronze: gold for jewellery, silver for both jewellery and finer table service, and bronze for jewellery and everyday tableware.

For large-scale construction projects, potters might have produced the bricks and tiles, working co-operatively with brick-makers, due to their convergent requirements for clay and firing kilns. The construction trades included the woodworkers, brick- and tile-workers, metalworkers and stonemasons who contracted with municipal, provincial and imperial potentates to build public and private edifices. Construction workers also applied themselves to infrastructure projects to build and repair wharves, walls, towers, roads, bridges, cisterns and aqueducts.

With few exceptions, it was among these more modest and hard-working people that Christianity took root and flourished. The tradition of Greek saint stories informs us that the family of Nicholas made a comfortable living among the Christians of Patara who worked at trades and crafts. His family brought him up in the way of the Christian faith and in communion with the Church.

There is no physical description of Nicholas, but we can assume that he probably had dark hair. He would have worn the child's costume of the day—a cotton or wool tunic that was short-sleeved and knee-length—and either sandals or shoes of leather. Nicholas probably lived very much like the other children in his town. He attended school at one of the market squares, or agorae, and studied under the instruction of a pedagogue. Nicholas studied his lessons in grammar, arithmetic and reading in Greek. He probably had friends with whom he played board games, ball games, hide-and-seek and pretend games with toys fashioned from wood, bone, clay or cloth. He and his family visited with their neighbours and enjoyed dinner parties and picnics together. These visits were occasions for entertainments such as storytelling, singing and playing music.[8]

Nicholas' family attended church on Sunday and brought him up to understand the Scriptures and worship. The small town church that they attended had probably been adapted from a house, shop or storehouse. Although humble, like other Christian churches of the late third century, its walls were likely decorated with scenes from the Old Testament and the Gospels. Nicholas might have seen Daniel facing the lions, as well as Noah and all the animals in his Ark from the Old Testament, and Jesus in a boat with the fishermen from the Gospels.[9]

In the generation of Nicholas' parents, the Emperor Valerian had, at first, acted benevolently towards the Christians. Later in his reign, Valerian turned against his Christian subjects and took up the cause of persecution. He raged against the Christians, calling upon his provincial magistrates and their Hellenist friends in the East to inflict damage on the churches and their leaders. This rampage ended when the Persians took Valerian prisoner. His son Gallienus took over as sole emperor in 261; he restored tolerance towards the Christians and even went so far as to rebuild their places of worship.

The Christian adults around Nicholas remembered the persecution under Valerian, and this made them cautious, private and close-knit as a community. They were especially protective towards each other and their children. It was in the midst of this community of Christians that Nicholas made formative preparations to become a priest. Their wariness about the Hellenists, Roman imperial functionaries among the Greeks in the East, inculcated in Nicholas the skills that he would later draw upon to nurture and protect his community of Christians. The Christians of Patara kept informed about the state of the world by listening to the stories of events in the Empire that circulated with the travellers at the docks and on the roads.

The Greek tradition informs us that the family of Nicholas recognized early his unique spiritual gifts. Nicholas' pastor encouraged him to become a priest, and a senior priest mentored him in his preparation. Christian Scriptures, faith and worship provided Nicholas with the necessary resources in his formation as a person of faith and as a student of divinity. Greek language and learning provided him with the foundation in grammar, rhetoric and philosophy that he needed in order to study for the priesthood. When he became a priest under a senior priest's supervision, people in the Church observed that Nicholas would be a luminary among pastors.[10]

The Greek stories tell us that the teachings Nicholas learned in the Church stimulated his mind and caused him to thirst for more knowledge of the truths of the Christian faith. In the late third century, Christian writings included *The Didache*, or "The Teaching," which was a document at least as old as the Gospels and the Letters of the Apostles. *The Didache* was a short manual in two parts—part one presented a lesson on the two ways of life or death, and part two served as a guide for Christian worship and community, and ended with a warning to be prepared for Christ's return. *The Didache* circulated widely around the eastern Mediterranean basin, and Nicholas probably felt the influence of its lessons and examples.

Nicholas and other Christian youths would have learned from *The Didache* about the decision to live a life inspired by love rather than one ruled by ignorance, and how to conduct worship and life in the community. The text on the two ways of life or death provided a practical guide for moral living based on the teachings of Christ. Among the moral admonitions are, first, to follow the two greatest commandments and, second, to refuse anything that has been offered to a pagan deity.

The Didache sets forth the two greatest commandments: You shall love the Lord your God with all your heart, and with all your soul, and with all your mind. You shall love your neighbour as yourself (Matthew 22:37-40). "The way of life" then issues from the two commandments, and lists examples of how to follow them. Among the teachings that Nicholas and fellow Christians derived from "the way of life," and that follow the first of the two greatest commandments, are these: to pray for persecutors and to give freely to anyone in need.

Nicholas and other Christians learned from *The Didache* to refuse any item that came from a pagan offering. The point of the lesson was clear: when Christians refused to have anything to do with an offering to another deity, they proved the purity of their love for God. In the late third century, *The Didache* was about 200 years old. In its admonition about offering to pagan idols, however, *The Didache* anticipated trials yet to come, and prepared Nicholas and other Christians to face them.[11]

By following the dictates of their faith, the Christians set themselves apart from their Hellenistic neighbours in their manner of living. For example, while the pagan citizens of Patara enjoyed the diversions offered at the theatre, Christians and their families, like that of Nicholas, avoided them. The performances in the Greek theatres of the East during the late third century had changed from the literary to the libidinal. The more popular programs were pantomimes, in which both female and male actors, musicians, singers and dancers produced the effect of a variety show. Visual effects and stage settings included vivid scenic backdrops, and actors flying over the stage suspended on ropes. From a Christian perspective, theatre programs too often took on a bawdy or obscene character, inciting the audiences to behave in a raucous and offensive manner.

The Christian residents of Patara preferred the more satisfying pleasures of walking in gardens, reading, composing devotional songs, socializing with their Christian and non-Christian friends, picnicking, and playing games and sports. Many Patarans had gardens that were connected to the house, giving an effect of indoor-outdoor living. They spent as much time in their gardens as their lifestyle allowed, using their gardens as a place to read, sing and play music, and hold dinner parties in the open air.[12]

Christians renewed themselves by attending a worship service called the "liturgy," and by praying. The prayer regimen that the presbyters, or church elders, recommended to the faithful called for prayers every three hours throughout each day, beginning at sunrise. Christians also received guidance to attend church every day, although in practice, many attended only a weekly liturgy and devotions on feast days.[13]

The residents of Patara were part of the greater cultural entity of the Roman Empire. Citizens of the Roman Empire shared a universal political culture, no matter where they resided. The citizen of Alexandria in Egypt possessed the same rights and privileges, such as access to infrastructure, the justice system and property rights for women and men, and observed the same imperial conventions of public decorum and activity as the citizen's counterpart in Rome.

The universality of imperial culture in the East, however, did not extend beyond the official centres of Roman administration and custom. Throughout the Empire, the settled cultures of the West and East differed substantially. In the West, which consisted of Britain, Gaul, Spain, Africa, Italy and the western Balkans, residents spoke the official language of Latin. By contrast, in the East, which included the eastern Balkans, Greece, Asia Minor, Syria, Palestine and Egypt, residents spoke the official language of Greek. The language difference between the Latin West and the Greek East was the most obvious sign of a more fundamental difference in cultures.

The West identified with so-called masculine psychological principles, and the East with feminine ones, a distinction in psyches that grew from elements of traditions and beliefs. In the Latin mythology of the West, the more popular stories emphasized male heroes and their masterful qualities. Jupiter and Hercules were the father-and-son team of gods whose feats of strength and power awed the Romans, so much so that, in the year 285, the Emperor Diocletian named Jupiter as patron of his rule, and Hercules as patron of his subordinate Caesar Maximian. By contrast, the Greek mythology of the East celebrated female deities and their splendid qualities. For example, stories depicting the wisdom and warrior prowess of the goddess Athena, and exploits of the huntress, moon and fertility goddess Artemis inspired pagans of the East to worship them.[14]

The vastness and complexity of the Empire as it approached the fourth century led the Emperor Diocletian in the years 286 to 293 to introduce measures that he hoped would increase the efficiency of its administration. He split the Empire in two, forming halves in the West and East, and placed a tetrarchy, a group of four leaders, in power. The tetrarchy consisted of Diocletian himself as primary augustus in the East with a subordinate augustus in the West, and two caesars, one serving each augustus. Diocletian's political division of the Empire followed roughly the demarcation between the Eastern and Western cultural hemispheres, with the augustus of the West and his caesar ruling everything west of the eastern Balkans, and the augustus of the East and his caesar ruling everything east of the western Balkans.[15]

The Empire had another inherent division as well as those of language and mythology—in the distribution of wealth. A small group of rich and prominent families lived supremely over another small group of lower-middle-class merchants and artisans who lived significantly better than a vast underclass of poor shopkeepers and labourers. Nicholas' family would have been in the class of the merchants and artisans. In a typical provincial town such as Patara, exquisitely attired people from wealthy families would parade the streets in style hastily pursued by their entourage, passing the humble yet colourful shops and storehouses of workers in trades and crafts who paid rents to the same rich passers-by. The wealthy of Patara would have followed the custom set by Rome for its high-born citizens, by providing an occasional gift to the city, such as a new civic building, road, bridge or wharf. The city councils made a public event of such gifts, both to acknowledge the celebrated donor and to encourage other potential donors.

The special and occasional nature of gifts to the city from its wealthy patronesses and patrons benefited only a small number of residents at any particular time. Little in such giving did much to salve the human wreckage that lined the streets of every city in the Empire of the late third century. Except for an occasional public gift of food, goods or economic relief, the multitude of urban poor lived each day hand to mouth with no hope of improving their situation.

The huge gap between rich and poor originated with the pattern of ownership of agricultural land, for agriculture was the basis of the Roman economy. A few important and very wealthy families owned vast agricultural estates and, therefore, most of the land capable of producing new wealth. By controlling the lands, the high-born families controlled the wealth of the Empire. That part of the wealth that flowed beyond the grasp of high-born families went to a thinly populated class of merchants and artisans—such as the family of Nicholas—who made moderate incomes and, lastly, to a multitude of labourers and others who lived in abject poverty. The imperial and provincial governments offered no regular social services programs—people simply had to take care of themselves or starve.[16]

Into that abyss of human need, ignored by provincial and imperial authorities, stepped the Christian communities. Led by bishops, priests, deaconesses and deacons, the faithful carried out their ministry to the urban poor. The Christian churches of the first four centuries provided hospice care for the sick, as well as support for widows, orphans and the unfortunate. Christians followed the unique Jewish practice of regularizing benevolence and cultivating solidarity within their congregations. From the teachings in the Gospels, the Christians, and young Nicholas with them, cultivated a strong sense of responsibility to care for the souls and bodies of those in need.

Chapter 2

Priest Nicholas and the Christian Community

Nicholas was now a young man ready to take his place as an adult member of the community. His experiences as a youth in Patara among his Christian friends and family had instilled in him a devout love of God and an exceptional depth of spirit. We learn from the Greek tradition of his natural inclination towards generosity and kindness. As a young adult, Nicholas fully embraced the vocation of priest, knowing full well the risks and sacrifices that might be required of him.[17]

Christian priests in the late third century typically drew on a common set of skills and principles that they acquired through both classical and Christian studies. To prepare himself for the priesthood, Nicholas probably sought higher education in rhetoric and philosophy at a nearby centre for learning, studied a number of Christian texts and possibly even travelled to Jerusalem in order to, literally, walk in the way of Christ. Nicholas' studies and travels would have gradually deepened his wisdom, shaping him into a highly respected and much-loved man with great spiritual authority based on his actions of love and justice.[18]

If Nicholas sought higher education and followed the pattern of other students in the Eastern Roman Empire, he would have travelled to where the program of study was being offered. The search for higher education in the East brought students to one of the great cities to pursue their studies with an eminent professor at a well-established centre for learning. For example, one promising student, Gregory of Neo-Caesarea in Asia Minor, with his brother, Athenodorus, had gone to Berytus, Syria, to study law at the famous centre for legal study. Not long after starting their studies, they learned exciting news: the great Christian teacher of philosophy, Origen, had come to nearby Caesarea in Palestine. They travelled to Caesarea to hear Origen, then stayed under his instruction for five years, during which time they abandoned law for philosophy and paganism for Christianity. Gregory eventually became the celebrated Bishop of Neo-Caesarea, who served in the last half of the third century. He, like other Christian commentators who wrote in Greek during his time, employed Greek philosophy in the service of the Gospel message.[19]

Depending on his family's financial condition, Nicholas might have studied at one of the centres for learning in Asia Minor. It was important for him to understand rhetoric and philosophy so that, when required, he could hold his ground in disputes with the Hellenists. To reach his chosen centre of learning, Nicholas travelled either by land where passable roadways existed or by coastal sea routes where that was more practical.

People of all types travelled extensively throughout the Roman Empire in the time of Nicholas. By land, they could travel the well-developed system of roadways that both provincial and imperial authorities helped to maintain. Travellers could journey on foot or ride on an animal (a mule or donkey), and carry their own belongings in a bundle. Those who had means could arrange conveyance on a wheeled cart. By any mode of travel, a person who traversed a distance of 30 kilometres per day made good progress. Comfort was variable en route. Along some stretches of road, travellers enjoyed the hospitality of private inns and the security of highway police, but on others, where accommodations and guard stations were scarce, travellers faced inconvenience and possibly even danger.

Where travel overland was too arduous, the traveller could choose to sail on one of the thousands of mercantile ships that voyaged to hundreds of Mediterranean ports. Among the grander of these far-flung ports were Ostia for Rome, Piraeus for Athens and Caesarea for Jerusalem, as well as the ports of Thessalonica, Ephesus, Alexandria and Antioch. Merchant ships accepted passengers only if they had room—captains gave priority to cargo rather than comfort. Travellers on such vessels had to make do by improvising as comfortable a berth as possible on the open deck. They had to bring their own food and to settle themselves amid the rigging of the ship, bundles of goods and other passengers who had claimed deck space.

Like their counterparts on the highways, travellers on merchant ships faced certain risks in voyaging. These ranged from muscle cramps, seasickness, minor injury and petty theft to being stranded or overtaken by pirates, shipwrecked and drowned. The benefits of sea travel included speed and assurance—speed in that even a slow sail was usually faster than a trek on land, and assurance that the ship's company observed a social hierarchy that encouraged order and predictability. More experienced travellers would have arranged to sail with a veteran captain and seasoned crew.

Some of the best mariners were of Phoenician heritage from Syria, Palestine and Egypt. Their mastery of navigation on the Mediterranean Sea was legendary. They designed and sailed the lateen-rigged sailing ships, which had a triangular sail on a long yard set at a 45-degree angle to the mast. Lateen-rigged merchant ships plied the Mediterranean Sea in great numbers from the second century into the fourth. The Phoenicians were justly proud of this tradition, which formed part of the foundational knowledge for their later accomplishments in mathematics and the sciences.[20]

Wherever Nicholas might have travelled to obtain learning, he probably returned to Patara for further pastoral study under his senior priest's tutelage. Nicholas' mentor, a Christian cleric, could have taught him the scriptural, liturgical and pastoral skills he needed to prepare for Christian priesthood. By the late third century, a rich literary tradition was available to aid Nicholas in his development as a priest. Nicholas would have studied, in his native Greek language, the Septuagint Old Testament, the Gospels and the Epistles, as well as classic Christian writings that circulated widely. He would have learned the beliefs and practice of the faith by reading the popular Christian forerunners: Clement of Rome, Ignatius of Antioch and Polycarp of Smyrna. He would have known *The Didache*, a composite manual of Christian ethical teachings and worship instructions that was widely available in the East.[21]

The Christian forerunners were of inestimable value to Christians of the fourth century. These post-apostolic leaders of the Church provided Christians with guidance in applying principles from the Scriptures to their lives, and with a connection and sense of continuity with Christians who had gone before. From their writings, Nicholas would have gained insights into the traditions of the Church and the experiences of its pastors that he could then apply to his formation as a priest.

Clement of Rome wrote a letter to the church of Corinth at the end of the first century. In his letter, he urged the Christians there to overcome their disputes and failures by remembering their past victories in faith as members of one of the Apostle Paul's original churches. Employing examples from both the Scriptures and philosophy, Clement asked the faithful at Corinth to abandon mischief and renew their commitment to Christian community. He urged the Corinthians once again to order their lives according to the teachings of Christ, to practise charity and humility, and to reunite in agreement around the Gospels and the order of worship. Clement's letter to the church of Corinth, which had been much copied and circulated among the churches of the Empire, began to advance the organizational doctrines of the apostolic succession of bishops, and the authority of bishops and clergy over laypersons.[22]

Ignatius of Antioch wrote seven letters to churches in cities along his route while he traversed Asia Minor as a prisoner. An imperial tribunal had condemned him for his Christian religious views in his home city, under persecution by the Emperor Trajan in about the year 116. Roman soldiers transported him across Asia Minor to Rome for his execution. In his letters, Ignatius spoke poetically of his approaching death and martyrdom. Throughout his letters, Ignatius repeatedly warned the faithful against the heresy of Docetism, from the Greek *doke*, meaning a "vision," which proposed that Jesus Christ merely *seemed* to be a mortal man. Ignatius reasserted the full humanity of Christ. Ignatius, like Clement, called upon Christians to obey the authority of their bishops—to be in tune with their bishops as strings to a harp.

Polycarp of Smyrna was a follower of the Apostle John, who appointed him to the post of Bishop of Smyrna. Irenaeus, a later friend of Polycarp, described him as a valued witness to the teachings of the original Apostles. Living to a great age, Polycarp shared the wisdom and richness of his years in his letter to the church at Philippi. In that letter, Polycarp encouraged the faithful to remember the ways of the faith, to apply themselves earnestly to them and to their vocations in the Church. He asked the Christians at Philippi to turn their anger at a faulted priest and presbytera into a prayerful effort to help restore the two individuals to full communion. In the account of the martyrdom of Polycarp preserved by Irenaeus, Polycarp provided the example of a believer with resolute and empowering faith in the promise of the Gospel.

Priest Nicholas might have studied Polycarp's advice for building a pastor's character, which Polycarp offered to the clergy in his well-circulated second-century letter to the Christians of Philippi. Polycarp said that the cleric should have a great capacity for sympathy and compassion towards humankind. He described the pastor's concern for reclaiming those who have become lost and alienated, or who are ill. The provider of care must help widows, orphans and others who are needy. Polycarp also advised the cleric to engage in those things that are honourable before God and people. A pastor must guard against anger, favour or unfairness, and must repel any impulse to acquire money. Polycarp reminded Christians to refrain from judging and criticizing, as none are without fault. He reminded the faithful that those who seek to have God forgive their misdeeds must also forgive others because all live under God's economy and Christ's judgment. Polycarp urged that all who serve the Church do so with the awe and reverence exemplified by Jesus Christ, the Apostles and the Prophets. Nicholas demonstrated his possession of the graces of a priest that Polycarp had described.[23]

With the letters of Polycarp and the other Christian forerunners, lessons from *The Didache*, the Gospels, the Letters and the Old Testament, Nicholas found the font for priestly character formation and pastoral skills. These sources, readily available to him during his youth, would have helped him to prepare for his journey to become Bishop of Myra.

When Nicholas had completed his studies, he received his ordination to the Christian priesthood in Patara. Priests, like other people in the towns and cities of the Eastern Roman Empire, wore tunics. Nicholas would have worn a cotton or wool tunic with a small amount of decoration—perhaps borders, waistband and collar embroidered with Christian symbols—clothing that was not very different from the clerical attire priests wear today. In appearance, Nicholas resembled his fourth-century Greek countrymen, and would have been barely over five feet tall, with dark hair and a slight build. His presence would have been that of a prayerful and devout servant of God.

In the cities of the Roman Empire, provincial and imperial authorities most often ignored the needs of the unfortunate, while Christian communities eagerly provided for them. Led by bishops, priests, deaconesses and deacons, the faithful carried out their ministry to the urban poor in the manner described in Acts 4:

> Now the company of those who believed were of one heart and soul, and no one said that any of the things which he possessed was his own, but they had everything in common. And with great power the Apostles gave their testimony to the resurrection of the Lord Jesus, and great grace was upon them all. There was not a needy person among them, for as many as were possessors of lands or houses sold them, and brought the proceeds of what was sold and laid it at the Apostles' feet; and distribution was made to each as any had need (Acts 4:32-35).[24]

A Greek story claims that Nicholas had learned of an unfortunate family in Patara. This family had fallen on hard times and the father, a widower, was preparing to sell the children into slavery. Nicholas intervened anonymously by secretly leaving enough money at their home for the children to be spared. While this story describes Nicholas as a giver of gifts, it might have happened that Nicholas, as a Christian priest, would have performed many such acts of kindness to relieve many unfortunate families, and especially to rescue children, the most fragile of all. This was a moral obligation, particularly in view of the stark contrast between pagan and Christian values regarding children. An example of this contrast in values was the pagan practice of leaving unwanted newborn infants outside and exposed to the elements and the Christian abhorrence of such behaviour.[25]

Greek tradition is uncertain about whether Nicholas travelled from Patara to Jerusalem in the late third century to visit the holy sites. Yet many Christians in the third-century Roman Empire did make the pilgrimage to Palestine and the Holy Land. To make a pilgrimage to Jerusalem, a traveller would have sailed from Lycia aboard a merchant vessel, stopping at a few ports en route to Caesarea. The ship carrying the pilgrim would have sailed towards the harbour at Caesarea along a concrete seawall approximately 70 metres long, upon which stood stone buildings and towers. At the entrance of the harbour, six pagan deities greeted the arriving voyagers, in the form of two triads of great colossi, standing on huge stone platforms to each side. Within the harbour, the city came into view, splendidly adorned with Roman architecture that included a marketplace, amphitheatre and recital hall. High above all the rest stood the majestic temple dedicated to Caesar, inhabited by a colossus of Caesar Augustus.[26]

After a short stay in Caesarea, a traveller would have had to make a difficult five-day overland journey to Jerusalem, which would perhaps have progressed as follows.

> The pilgrim reached the edge of the market square and the entire panorama of Caesarea opened to view. Ahead was a wide, paved agora where four plateia met. In the agora, merchants and artisans prepared their awning-draped stands for the day's transactions. Beyond the colourful linens of the market stalls loomed the massive walls, buildings and towers that enclosed the harbour.
>
> Out along the quay, labourers and mariners loaded and unloaded cargoes between ships, carts and mules. All this activity came under the wary eyes of soldiers who positioned themselves around the entire circumference of the harbour. In fact, everywhere the sojourner looked, at least one pair of soldiers stood guard.
>
> In the murky water of the harbour rested a host of ships that varied in size and purpose. Most were small, round-hulled and square-rigged or lateen-

rigged merchant ships, approximately 30 metres long, which were used for carrying goods such as grains, oil and wine. Also at anchor were long and sleek triremes, or war galleys, with three rows of oars on each side and sinister eyes painted on their hulls. On their prows jutted bronzed rams, sharp and deadly. The warships sat on the water like seabirds with wings furled, vigilant and rapacious.

The traveller considered how best to proceed overland to Jerusalem. According to local wisdom, it would be an arduous walk, a five-day journey through mountainous country. While eager to begin, the adventurer deemed it unwise to travel alone, and so decided to enquire locally about others who might be travelling that way.

The sojourner moved along the market square, paused among the sellers' stalls and walked amid the exotic displays of goods that took shape ahead. The sellers filled their stands with every shape, size and colour of local produce, herbs, oils, wines, along with splendid wares of shimmering glass and gleaming metal. The visitor moved on to the fabric dealers' stalls, where satins and linens of the finest weaves in brilliant reds and purples billowed and beckoned in the sea breezes.

At last, a wool merchant directed the pilgrim to a caravan of wool suppliers who planned to leave that evening for Jerusalem. The traveller struck a bargain with them and made arrangements to join their caravan at sunset.

At the appointed time, the adventurer left Caesarea with the caravan and crossed the Plain of Sharon over to Gitta, a village in the foothills along the river, then across to Yishub, where they rested for the day. The second evening brought them to Sebaste. On the third night they reached Manayim, and on the fourth, Ephraim. They travelled overnight on the fifth night and caught sight of Jerusalem at daybreak.

The caravan approached the fabled walls of Jerusalem from the north, having travelled for a while along the spine of the mountains. Nothing could have prepared the sojourner for the vision ahead—a proud mountain crowned gloriously with a golden city. In the early morning light, Jerusalem bore the shape and beauty of a rose – indeed, a rose in full bloom, yet one composed in gilded stone.

In Jerusalem, the pilgrim walked with wonder in the way of Christ on his path from birth to death and to life again...

During a voyage as arduous as the one to Caesarea and back to Lycia, the traveller would have faced the same dangers as others who braved the Mediterranean Sea. One first-century voyager, the Apostle Paul, experienced this calamity in the eastern Mediterranean:

> And when the south wind blew gently, supposing that they [the mariners] had obtained their purpose, they weighed anchor and sailed along Crete, close inshore. But soon a tempestuous wind, called the northeaster, struck from the land; and when the ship was caught and could not face the wind, we gave way to it and were driven. And running under the lee of a small island called Cauda, we managed with difficulty to secure the boat; after hoisting it up, they took measures to undergird the ship; then, fearing that they should run on the Syrtis, they lowered the gear and so were driven. As we were violently storm-tossed, they began next day to throw the cargo overboard; and the third day they cast out with their own hands the tackle of the ship. And when neither sun nor stars appeared for many a day, and no small tempest lay on us, all hope of our being saved was at last abandoned (Acts 27:13-20).[27]

At Patara, Priest Nicholas and his fellow Christians would have gathered together into communion in the spirit of *The Didache*. They would have blessed and taken bread and wine, so that they would join with Christ as he was joined with God. The Christians at the time of Nicholas believed, in accordance with *The Didache*, that, just as human hands produced a loaf of bread from the grains that grew in the fields and drew wine from the grapes that ripened in the vineyards, as many separate fruits became one in the bread and wine, so did the faithful commune at the Eucharist into oneness with Christ. In the Gospels, Jesus Christ had assured the Apostles that their faith would fasten them like branches of a vine to him, who was the "true vine" joined with God (John 15:1-8). The Christians of the fourth century emulated the Apostles in the hope that, by faith expressed in devotion, prayer, service and communion with his Church, they too would be fastened as branches to the vine of Christ and thereby to God.[28]

Worship and communion with the Church brought the faithful together into a variety of shelters. There were few dedicated church buildings in the early fourth century. Such buildings were recent constructions, at a time when the majority of worshippers still met either in house churches or converted shops and storehouses. These adapted churches, while simple and humble, often featured decorations in paint or mosaic tiles of scenes from the Old Testament, which was the cultural legacy that Christians inherited from the Jewish synagogues. Old Testament themes of house church art included Adam and Eve, Noah and the Ark, Abraham preparing to sacrifice Isaac, Moses striking the rock to draw water, Jonah and the whale, Daniel in the lion's den, and the three youths in the fiery furnace.

Christian artists also added New Testament themes to depict events from the life of Christ. New Testament images on house church walls included the baptism of

Christ, Jesus healing the paralytic, the Samaritan woman with Jesus at the well, Christ raising Lazarus to life, and the Apostle Peter walking on water with the help of Jesus.[29]

The first dedicated church buildings grew up in the larger cities such as Rome, Athens, Alexandria, Antioch and Jerusalem. Christian artisans modelled their first church buildings after the design of the basilica, which provided a solid and open interior space for public buildings. Some of the larger church buildings provided additional enclosures for the clergy and their ministries to the city. For example, by the middle of the third century, the church of Rome was able to house a staff of almost 200 clergy and to provide financial support for about 1500 widows and poor. The churches in the grander cities became mother churches to most of Christendom.[30]

In the church celebration of public worship, known in Greek as the *liturgia,* Christians intoned prayers, chants and songs by voice only, never with musical instruments. Both women and men composed and voiced the chants and hymns. The earliest chants came to Christianity from the tradition of worship followed in the Jewish synagogues. The Christian worshippers borrowed the Hebrew word "Alleluia" in chants of praise for God. One pagan critic of Christianity, the second-century scholar Celsus, complained that the chants used in Christian worship were so exotic and beautiful that they caused in him an emotional sympathy, which annoyed him because he suspected that it dulled his capacity for critical thinking.

Three songs in particular that resounded in the time of Priest Nicholas were the joyous Greek hymn *You Have Found Your Bridegroom Christ*, the anapaestic hymn *Father, Son and Holy Spirit, Let All Creation Sing* and the cheerful *Hail Gladdening Light*.[31]

The Christian worshippers who sang those hymns lived in the city but disdained the overt paganism of city culture. The cities of the Empire boldly presented tableaux in stone of Roman and Greek deities in various heroic poses. Classical and imperial artisans emblazoned images and themes of the pantheon everywhere on public architecture. The Christians viewed the ornate pagan temples and tumultuous festivals with disgust. They preferred the simplicity and purity of their modest lives in Christian fellowship. They practised their faith in spite of the city rather than in concert with it.

Christians saw their cities as smouldering heaps of evil, rank with the odour of every human vice. By contrast, the countryside and provincial towns offered virtues in abundance. Saint Symeon the Fool commented that he had often seen local peasants entering the city to worship in the church. He likened their kindness to purest gold and praised their industry in earning their own bread.[32]

The religious landscape of the Empire followed its economic structure. At the top of the economic hierarchy, the small group of wealthy families followed the prescribed state paganism, which was an extravaganza encompassing Roman and Greek deism and a melange of eastern mystery religions. Yet, in practice, the high-born pagans who had taken an interest in the lessons of their tutors in the classics embraced the almost monotheistic variants that their favourite philosophers had distilled through inquiry. The small group of lower-middle-class merchants and artisans, who occupied the next lower level of the economic hierarchy, also conformed to the state religion, except for those few who retained deities from their homelands, or Judaism or Christianity. The vast underclass of poor shopkeepers and labourers flocked around the imperial paganism, except a minority of those who had brought their own beliefs with them from the far-flung outposts of the Empire, were Jews or had become Christians. Based on this composition of the religions in the Empire, Christians probably numbered five per cent, or about 2.5 million souls, of the Roman Empire's approximately 50 million people.[33]

The Christian community that nurtured Nicholas to priesthood maintained the early forms and precepts of the faith from its sources: the Apostles, Judaism and Hellenism. In private home, shop and storehouse, or dedicated church, the faithful gathered to worship and to celebrate their union with Christ in the communal meal of bread and wine. The Christians inherited a tradition that the imperial authorities viewed as a suspect innovation and that pagan commentators considered a curious novelty. The Christian historian Eusebius of Caesarea in the fourth century credited Philo with describing

Christians using the Greek *therapeutrides* for the women and *therapeutae* for the men. Eusebius wanted to show that Christians, like physicians, cured the souls of those who sought their help or, as servants, rendered selfless service to others. Whether Eusebius cited Philo correctly or not, the importance Eusebius placed on these roles for Christians served to illustrate the importance they placed upon the condition of a soul and the joy of service to others.[34]

The Apostles gave fourth-century Christians the Gospels and the Letters, which were the scriptural treasury from which Christians in the time of Nicholas drew their inspiration and tradition of worship. Judaism provided the Christians with both the Old Testament and, from its commentaries, a sense of how to understand the spiritual struggle in a hostile world. Hellenism, which was the fabric of that hostile world, also supplied the philosophical and rhetorical threads that Priest Nicholas and other Christians used in their struggle against usurpers from without and rebels from within their ranks.

Native Greek scholars were not the only ones who valued Greek philosophy. Latin Romans savoured Greek philosophy with enthusiasm comparable to that of native Greeks. In the years when Diocletian reigned (284–305), Romans especially liked the philosophy of Plato. Pagan commentators invoked Plato in tracts aimed at urging citizens to return to worship of the ancient deities of Rome. Many of the pagan advocates of the pantheon, or family of Graeco-Roman deities, wrote treatises against the Christian faith. For a time, scholars from either margin of the religious divide engaged in a polite rhetorical contest. A pamphlet skirmish between the pagans and Christians generated copies for circulation throughout the ports of call in the Roman world. Two notable opponents, the pagan philosopher Porphyry of Sicily and the Christian rhetorician Lactantius of Bithynia, provided volumes of philosophical debate that were available to any interested provincial within a few kilometres of a Mediterranean harbour.[35]

The central question of the arguments between the Neoplatonists and the Christians was this: How could one approach God? The pagan philosophers, notably Porphyry, argued that it was possible for a person to attain the heights of wisdom and nearness to God through contemplation of the divine. The Neoplatonists devised elaborate allegorical descriptions of the realms of heaven and the orbits therein, and of the journeys one must make in order to ascend to those esoteric heights of knowing. The pagan intellectuals approached God with their minds, while the Christians approached God with their hearts. The Christians, especially Lactantius, asserted that people require the help of God, by way of Jesus Christ, to transcend the limitations of temporal life and of human error, and that God invites every person to embrace a life inspired by love, which they express in devotion, prayer and service, in order to advance on the path that leads them to sanctity, in Greek *theosis*, and, ultimately, to blissful union with God.[36]

These discussions were highly technical in their philosophical content and allegorical description. They would not have had much impact upon anyone other than a small group of highly educated and well-read people. Yet, they formed the intellectual lines of force for events that occurred later, both in the reign of Diocletian and after his abdication. Pagans had been agitated enough with Christianity to launch a philosophical attack. Christians challenged the principles upon which state religion had been founded.

In this environment of cultural, philosophical and religious tensions, Priest Nicholas performed his duties as a pastor and watched and prayed. Christians of the fourth century rejected Graeco-Roman paganism as falling far short of the gifts of divine love and eternal life they received in the faith from the Apostles. These Christians held the hope that, by faith and in communion with Christ's Church, they would receive the Gospel promise of joyous union forever with Christ and God. The faithful gathered to worship in the manner described in *The Didache*. The instructions for worship called for Christians to assemble on the Lord's Day, traditionally Sunday, to make confession of their faults, to break bread and to make offering in the Eucharist.

CHAPTER 3

The New Bishop of Myra

According to the Greek stories, Nicholas served for a few years as a priest in Patara and then moved 50 kilometres east to Myra, the provincial capital of Lycia. The overland journey from Patara to Myra was prohibitively difficult because the way traced a lonely, narrow, rock-strewn path that wandered through the Taurus Mountains with many steep drops and frequent rock slides. That trek required a treacherous, five-day climb over the mountains.

A much easier route would have been to voyage from Patara east to Myra in a sailing ship. If Priest Nicholas chose to travel to Myra by sailing, his voyage might have proceeded as follows.

> The two mariners brought the traveller aboard their sailing skiff well before dawn, while it was still quite dark. Since other craft were heading out

for a day of fishing, the skiff and its occupants were of little interest to the guards, who were weary from their night watch.

The sailors, under the guise of preparing for a fishing trip, pulled up and mended one of the nets. Their little craft slipped away towards the first rays of dawn and, for the voyager, to an unknown destiny that offered more danger than promise.

The seafarer watched the silhouettes of the mountains as they approached and receded. Some were connected to the mainland, while others stood in the sea like great colossi. As mere shapes of stone, these forms were devoid of either power or personality. Yet the observer understood how more temporal minds could imbue such shapes with life.

The emigrant thought about what lay ahead in Myra. How would the people at Myra receive this stranger? Who could the newly arrived trust?

For two days they sailed, watchful for any signs of danger from the rocks that lay hidden along the jagged coast or from vessels that might loom across their path. At last, they rounded the last formation of rocks and caught sight of the opening to the Androkos River. The view of the shimmering river flowing proudly between two high promontories was majestic. The traveller found the panorama captivating, and rapt in wonder, was slow to notice the militia watch stations that were perched at the highest points on either side of the river.

The mariners positioned their craft so that it blended into the arc of vessels entering the mouth of the river. The militia guards watched attentively, but raised no alarms. Just inside the entrance and to the right, the sailors saw the docks for the imperial grain depot at Andriaki, a merchant outpost that supported considerable commerce in eastern grains and local commodities. Fortunately for the voyagers, other, much larger, ships had anchored near the arched stone granary warehouses.

Passing the stone arches and piers of the Empire's depot, the sailors in their tiny vessel could hear the crew members moving about the ships and quay. Eastern workers loaded amphorae and wooden barrels onto a pair of merchant ships. Buyers, sellers and officials bantered and laughed; the soldiers watched grimly. A warship lay at anchor nearby. Its prow jutted menacingly out towards the channel. Fortunately for the voyagers, there was sufficient commotion at Andriacus to distract the soldiers from taking much notice of them.

The visitor and the sailors felt reassured of their safe entrance as they pressed on into a great and lush valley, which lay sleepily like a child at the feet of its parent mountains. The mariners furled the sail and worked the oars as they approached the outskirts of Myra. Like the valley in which it was sheltered, Myra appeared to be a grand and lovely city.

There, at the base of the Taurus Mountains, caressed by the shifting Androkos River, was Myra. Larger than Patara, Myra could have supported 50,000 residents. The city lay in a valley that formed a half-circle more than 10 kilometres across, arced by the stony mountains and decorated with a golden hem of sand where it met the sapphire-hued Mediterranean Sea. Looking north from the sea, Myra's municipal, commercial and residential buildings stood bleached in the pale yellow of sunlight, and dappled generously with the rich greens and vibrant reds of floral cascades, fruit vines and trees. The amphitheatre stood grandly in a niche at the rocky foot of one of the mountains, and offered 35 rows of seats that spanned a distance of nearly 200 metres, all of it decorated in bas-relief with masks and garlands.

The traveller and the mariners approached a pier at a discrete block of buildings and fastened the skiff. The voyager gave them a blessing for their safe return and asked to take leave of them. As the two sailors rowed the skiff away towards the sea, the sojourner turned to what lay ahead...

The Greek tradition holds that Nicholas came to Myra to offer his life in service to the church. The presbyters of the church elected Nicholas to be their bishop, *episkopos* in Greek, which means, literally, "overseer." Then, as Bishop Nicholas, he guided the faithful of Myra as they faced the overwhelming storm of wrath that would soon bear upon the Christians of the East.[37]

In the three decades of Nicholas' life, Christians had enjoyed peace and justice even though the Roman Empire had not accepted Christianity as a legitimate religion. The imperial courts of Diocletian employed Christians in the highest offices, some within the emperor's own palace and in his personal entourage. Christians were even in charge of the management of the palace, including Diocletian's personal treasury.[38]

Similarly, the Empire, from the emperor down to the provincial magistrates, conferred respect upon the bishops in their cities. This was due, in part, to the precedents that Roman administration had recorded, where bishops had contributed to settling disputes and helping to maintain civil calm. Like other bishops, Bishop Nicholas was responsible for the spiritual direction and advocacy of his community. As an inheritor of the apostolic succession—one in the continuous chain of sanctified Apostles of Christ that Clement of Rome described in his first-century Letter to the Corinthians—Bishop Nicholas received by ordination a sacred charge to oversee the spiritual life of his diocese. As a protector of his people,

Bishop Nicholas also performed a vital public role as an advocate for the rights of Christians in a political environment dominated by self-interested Hellenists.[39]

One notable example of the political skill of bishops was the case of Paul of Samosata. After Bishop Demetrian died at Antioch, the presbyters granted the title of bishop to Paul of Samosata. By the year 264, Paul caused the other bishops in the East to doubt his orthodoxy and to suspect him of holding the belief that Christ had a fully human nature but not a divine one. The bishops of the East held a synod at Antioch to address the situation. Most were able to attend and they descended upon Antioch in force. Dionysius of Alexandria was unable to attend because of his advanced age and frail health, yet he sent a letter explaining his thoughts on the issue.

The bishops met in several sessions, attempting, through interviews with Paul and his associates, to fathom the extent of his heterodoxy, but to no avail. Paul and his friends were too adept at discussion to be cornered on any particular point in question.

While all the investigations of Paul in Antioch were in progress, other events ensued. Bishop Dionysius died, after having led the church at Alexandria for 17 years, and was replaced by Bishop Maximus. The Emperor Gallienus, having served for 15 years, was replaced by Claudius, who reigned for two years and then left his throne to Aurelian.

Under the reign of Aurelian, the synod of bishops held a final meeting in Antioch. The meeting was well attended and, this time, the bishops found their champion in Malchion, a presbyter who was the headmaster of an important Hellenic school of rhetoric in Antioch. He had arranged for a staff of shorthand writers to take notes while he defeated Paul of Samosata in a theological argument. Malchion handed the bishops their first victory over Paul, whom they excommunicated from the Church on grounds of heresy.

The synod of bishops drafted a letter explaining their concerted judgment and addressed it to Bishop Dionysius of Rome and Bishop Maximus of Alexandria, and distributed it to the provincial sees of the Empire. The letter further elaborated on the trouble that Paul had caused them, his heterodox beliefs and his misdeeds in life.

The bishops had removed Paul's title of bishop and his communion with the Church, but they had yet to remove Paul himself. Paul refused to surrender the church building. The synod of bishops appealed to the Emperor Aurelian, who responded with an order that handed them their second victory over Paul of Samosata. Aurelian ordered that the church building be placed in the possession of the Antiochian presbyters who were in receipt of the letter of authorization from the Bishop of Rome. Thus the city police came and evicted Paul from the church.[40]

By removing Paul from the see of Antioch, the bishops eased the instability in the East, which had been exacerbated by the disturbances around him. The bishops presented the Emperor Aurelian with a happy solution to a politically thorny problem that had put him at odds with Queen Zenobia, ruler of the eastern provinces in Asia Minor, Syria, Palestine and Egypt. In successfully dealing with this and other challenges, the bishops had shown that they could discipline their own ranks and contribute to civil order.[41]

Another important reason why the Empire respected its bishops was that, for the most part, the bishops were well-educated and honourable people who enlisted the aid and support of informed and capable women and men. Thus had Christian bishops attained a status and level of respect equalling that of provincial magistrates. Along with this respect came the impression of legitimacy, leading the churches to ease into comfort. People came in greater numbers to associate with the churches and the faith. As a result, Christianity enjoyed a period of growth resulting in larger communities and more churches.

Such growth in the Christian churches, along with recent setbacks within the Empire, caused agitation among the pagans. By the fourth century, people throughout the Empire had begun to feel the cumulative effects of decades of instability. The foundation of support for the population of the Empire and the primary industry of Asia Minor, agriculture, had diminished in the wake of destruction and ravaging by Roman armies and barbarian invaders. Farm workers who had suffered the deprivations of these attacks moved to the towns and cities, where they either found work in the service of the wealthy Roman citizens or they became outlaws. Those who chose to exploit the Roman citizens banded together. For example, the Bacaudae formed a large force of rebels that operated in Gaul, and chose leaders whom they called "emperors."[42]

The imperial government took measures to remedy the diminished supply of farm labour by delivering to landowners a ready supply of barbarian prisoners of war. This was, however, too little too late, since, by the reign of Aurelian (270–275), the flow of tax revenues to the imperial treasury had slowed enough for the Empire to crack down on the local councils within those provinces and regions that were in arrears.[43]

The diminished capacity of agriculture brought on by decades of destruction contributed to widespread malnutrition, as well as an increase in the frequency and severity of famines and epidemics. As a result of these conditions, the birth rate and population of the Roman Empire during the early fourth century probably decreased somewhat from the levels of the prior two and a half centuries.[44]

These were the economic and social conditions that Nicholas faced when he became Bishop of Myra. Bishop Nicholas had the ultimate responsibility for both the spiritual and earthly welfare of the faithful in Myra. The overwhelming struggle and personal sacrifice required for Christians like Bishop Nicholas to provide for such needs, particularly during the years 303 to 305, was both heroic and holy. In those days, the local diocesan Church offered the only hope of care for the destitute and infirm, and for widows and orphans. Bishop Nicholas, with his priests, deaconesses and deacons, would have worked to exhaustion to care for all the needy and suffering people who came their way.

While Bishop Nicholas struggled to preserve the health and well-being of his diocese, the shadow of greed crept towards Myra to incite the pagans to attack the Christians. The shadow sprang from the court of Diocletian in Nicomedia, which, like the fabled Pandora's box, had allowed uncontrollable forces to ravage throughout the land.

Late in his reign, which lasted from 284 to 305, the Roman Augustus Emperor Diocletian turned against the Christian sect. This was the time when Bishop Nicholas began serving in Myra. Diocletian adhered to a policy of pagan traditionalism. He worshipped the Roman pantheon and believed that others should do the same—for the good of Diocletian and his Empire. During the winter of 302 to 303, Diocletian and his heir apparent, Galerius, met at the palace in Nicomedia to discuss in secret what they should do about the Christians. Galerius, hewn of coarser material than Diocletian and strongly influenced by his devoutly pagan mother Romula, pressed his view that the

Christians behaved as enemies of the state and that the primary augustus should deal with them accordingly. Diocletian consulted with his principal advisors among the pagan magistrates and military commanders, and finally sought an answer from the pagan ministers of Apollo.

The answer that Diocletian allegedly received from Apollo, by way of ministers of the pagan rites, was slow in coming. The Tages, or chief expert in the ancient Etruscan art of divination by liver inspection, had difficulty seeing the signs he sought in the cattle liver. Diocletian slaughtered one hapless beast after another, but their livers apparently revealed no signs. Christian attendants to Diocletian made the sign of the cross on their foreheads each time he sacrificed an animal. The Tages noticed their gestures and suspected that the Christians were preventing the spirits of Apollo from doing their work. When he explained this to Diocletian, the emperor flew into a rage and ordered that all present make a sacrifice to Apollo or suffer beatings and dismissal from service.

Ultimately, Diocletian sought the advice of the oracle of the Milesian Apollo. He sent one of his trusted fortune tellers to put forward to Apollo his question about the Christians. The minister returned from his mission and delivered Apollo's answer: The Christian God indeed opposed the Roman deities. Thus Diocletian came to see Christians as his enemies.

His decision made, Diocletian waited for the feast of the Termini on February 23 in 303 to begin his termination of Christianity. His first act of destruction was carried out against a church building in Nicomedia that stood in prominent view of his palace. The imperial prefect and his assistants, tribunes and officers of the treasury forced open the church doors, burnt the Scriptures and confiscated the furnishings. A contingent of praetorians equipped with siege implements then marched to the church and tore it down stone by stone.

Later in 303, Diocletian pressed into force an edict outlawing Christian communities in all the major cities throughout the Empire. His first of several imperial decrees against Christianity circulated to the deputy praetorian prefects in every administrative region, and ordered the authorities to destroy the Christian churches and to burn their sacred books. Diocletian's order also declared that Christians in imperial employment should lose everything, including their freedom, unless they abandoned faith in Christ and professed the state paganism. His next decrees ordered the authorities first to imprison the leaders of the churches everywhere, then to compel them by any means to offer sacrifice to the pagan deities.

In the days that followed, Diocletian's deputy praetorian prefects and the authorities in every province enforced his edict against the Christians in all the major cities throughout the Empire. The Hellenist magistrates of the East zealously carried out the imperial orders to imprison church leaders—bishops, priests, deaconesses and deacons—and to compel them to worship the pagan deities. In his role as *episkopos*, Nicholas stood against magistrates who pressed the imperial assault against Christians. From his youth, Bishop Nicholas had been prepared for trouble with the Hellenists, and so was prepared to resist their assaults peacefully and to protect his community of Christians.[45]

The most intense conflict in Nicholas' life as Bishop of Myra was his protracted struggle against the Hellenists who imprisoned him for his faith, about the year 305, under the Great Persecution of Diocletian. Greek tradition relates that the authorities arrested and imprisoned Bishop Nicholas with many others. The magistrates gave no regard for gender or age. Imprisonment was only the first cruelty Bishop Nicholas would have had to endure at the hands of imperial officials. He would also have faced their threats and coercions aimed at forcing him to demonstrate obedience to the state deities. When he refused, he would have been beaten or tortured and thrown back into prison. Under the edict, his church was probably destroyed, along with the holy books. Added to his suffering would have been the anguish Bishop Nicholas would have felt at being unable to minister personally to his community when they most needed his care.

In prison, Bishop Nicholas would have received only such food and water as his friends could smuggle in to him. He would have been almost completely cut off from his diocese and parish except for the comrades who shared his prison and those brave souls from outside who brought him food, water and news. These visitors to Nicholas placed themselves in mortal danger by defying the imperial orders against aiding the "atheists," that is, the Christian prisoners. The standing imperial orders demanded that anyone caught offering assistance to the condemned Christians was, likewise, to be seized and punished.

From what the Greek tradition tells us of Bishop Nicholas, we learn that while in prison he maintained his faith and encouraged those imprisoned with him. If he had sufficient strength of body while in captivity, he could have led his fellow Christian prisoners in prayer and worship. Bishop Nicholas survived his imprisonment and endured the brutal attempts by the authorities to force him into obedience to the state religion.

While destruction and persecution raged against Christians in the East, in the West, the subordinate Augustus Maximian in Italy and his Caesar Constantius in Gaul and Britain had also received their orders from the senior Augustus Diocletian. Maximian carried out his instructions throughout Italy, destroying both churches and Christians. In contrast, Constantius followed Diocletian's orders to the extent that he destroyed Christian churches, but he evidently did not destroy believers. So the Christians of Gaul and Britain enjoyed a measure of leniency under their Caesar Constantius. Constantius' son, Constantine, lived at the court of

Diocletian as an officer-in-training and as a guest of the household. Diocletian probably had taken Constantine under his palace roof to ensure the loyalty of his father Constantius.[46]

There is evidence that in the Western provinces ruled by Caesar Constantius, the administrations enforced only Diocletian's first edict. The other orders—that they dismiss and disenfranchise Christians in imperial employment, and that they imprison Christian leaders and then compel them by force to offer pagan sacrifice—have no historical support. The persecution lasted less than three years in the West. Augustus Maximian abdicated in 305 and the persecution ended with his departure. Constantius had shown restraint from the start of the persecution and did not carry it beyond 305.[47]

CHAPTER 4

The Great Persecution of the Christians

By the year 305, the persecution raged to its full fury throughout the East. It grew like a conflagration from its original source: Diocletian's palace at Nicomedia. Shortly after the destruction of the church at Nicomedia, two suspicious fires broke out in the palace and threatened Diocletian's life. Galerius, who had both the motive and the guile to personally arrange these mishaps, accused the Christians of setting the fires. Diocletian reached such a pitch of fear and rage that he let loose upon the Christians an assault of vengeance that resulted in the torture and death of many in the imperial household and service. From there, his anger flared out against the Christian community of Nicomedia. The leader of the destroyed church, Bishop Anthimus, met his death, and thousands of other Christians suffered at the hands of the imperial persecutors.[48]

In Asia Minor, Syria, Palestine and Egypt, the magistrates received Diocletian's orders and set to work condemning, imprisoning, torturing or killing Christians by the thousands. The judges and their guards inflicted upon these Christians the same and even more diabolical punishments for their refusals to pay obeisance to the imperial deities.[49]

In the midst of their sufferings, Bishop Nicholas and other Christian leaders encouraged the faithful of their dioceses to hold fast to their belief in God's dispensation through Christ. To understand what Bishop Nicholas and his fellow captives endured, we look to a first-hand account from one of his brother bishops. Phileas of Alexandria, in his letter to the believers in Thumis, Egypt, exemplified the courage of Christian leaders who both condemned the behaviour of their persecutors and encouraged the tenacity of the faithful. Phileas described the torments perpetrated by the governor and his soldiers against the Christians in Alexandria.

According to Phileas, attacks upon the Christians began with threats and were followed by beatings. The governor then had each prisoner bound to the fixtures of the court building with their limbs stretched for the time that they remained conscious. While the victims hung there, faint and wounded, the governor lectured each one in turn to persuade them to comply with the emperor's orders by denouncing their faith in Christ and paying obeisance to the state religion. When the victims were of no further use to the governor, he had the soldiers cut them loose and hurl them to the ground in the courtyard. Some died there, while others died later, after the soldiers dragged them across the ground and threw them into prison. Those who did not die in prison were once again ordered to either participate in the pagan sacrifice or be killed. Many chose death, and among them was Phileas. Thus did many Christians hold firm throughout the duration of their torments.[50]

Not all Christians, however, had the fortitude to defy the authorities; these Christians cowered before the threats and punishments of their persecutors. Some went into hiding, some moved to safer regions and others co-operated with the authorities in order to save themselves. Those Christians who capitulated to the magistrates by surrendering the Scriptures or church property received the label of *traditores*, or "traitors to Christ," from their more steadfast comrades.[51]

The magistrates in the Eastern Roman Empire perpetrated against Christian leaders incidents of violence that were especially zealous and severe. Sentences ranged from imprisonment or forced labour in the metal mines and stone quarries to torture and death. An eyewitness to the Great Persecution, Lactantius of Bithynia, described how the persecution raged throughout the East. The magistrates imposed pagan sacrifice at the temples upon everyone they could arrest. They filled the prisons. The judges perpetrated outlandish tortures. So that none could escape judgment, the magistrates set up sacrificial altars in the secretarial rooms and at the entrance to the tribunal. That way, anyone who approached the judge would have to offer sacrifice, as at a pagan temple. In the case of one church leader named Donatus, his persecutors inflicted nine separate tortures upon him during his six years of imprisonment.[52]

The motivations among the pagans for their violence towards the Christians differed from the published justifications, such as the Christians were "atheists." Superstition prevailed among the citizens of the Eastern Roman Empire, who genuinely feared for their own welfare and security as well as that of the state. They believed that the recent cycle of droughts, diseases, famines and military failures happened because they, as Romans, had failed to win the favour of the deities. In the midst of Roman efforts to prop up reverence for the ancient pantheon of deities and for officially recognized deities from other regions in the East, the Jews and Christians stood apart and alien. The Jews had won legal exemption from practice of the state religion by Roman law dating back to the second century BCE. It was almost by default that the pagan Romans suspected the Christians of causing both the displeasure of the deities and the attendant disasters in the Empire. So, to the pagans, the Christians represented a fundamental threat to the very security and well-being of the Empire.[53]

The men who launched the Great Persecution did not devote themselves to the high-minded Neoplatonist contemplations of Plotinus and Porphyry. On the contrary, Diocletian and Galerius came from peasant and barbarian stock, and they advanced through the military the hard way. In their view, they defended the Empire against those who threatened its security. In their minds, Christians who angered the imperial deities usurped the public welfare and made themselves enemies of the state.

Diocletian and Galerius harboured superstitions about the Christians, fearing that the deities would not co-operate unless the Christians sacrificed to them. These pagan emperors and their Christian subjects held in common the belief that supernatural forces control events on earth, but they differed in how they communicated with the divinity exercising those forces. Diocletian and Galerius believed that they could bargain with the deities, and could buy their benevolence towards the Empire by performing magic rituals such as sacrificing to the gods and goddesses. By contrast, the Christians respectfully asked God for what they wanted and, through prayer and fasting, hoped to become more sincere of heart.

Lactantius of Bithynia, the fourth-century Christian rhetorician, argued passionately in the *Divine Institutes* for the pagans to disavow the use of violence in the defence of their deities. He illustrated how ignorance and blindness to the truth allowed the torturer the delusion of being in the right. Lactantius challenged the pagans to abandon force and to take up philosophical debate.[54]

Lactantius' plea was lost on all but a few high-minded and educated citizens. Diocletian kept company with a few enlightened people in his court. By contrast, Galerius repelled persons of culture and attracted those who shared his baser tastes. Few in the company of either Diocletian or Galerius would have paid the text of Lactantius much heed. Ultimately though, Lactantius did make a friend from his service to the court of Diocletian.

The perpetrators relaxed the persecution somewhat in the year 311. After leading an eight-year rampage against the Christian communities in the East, the principal Augustus Galerius fell seriously ill. In 311, when his illness brought him to the point of desperation, he issued a letter to the magistrates in the East, calling for a change of policy towards the Christians. He asked that they be shown clemency and that they be allowed to rebuild and gather in their houses of worship. Galerius even asked the Christians to pray for his welfare and for that of the Empire.[55]

Maximinus Daia, caesar in the East, had already made up his mind about both Galerius and the Christians. He demonstrated an independent, perhaps inventive, turn of mind. He chose to feign co-operation with the order to relax the persecution, then to launch an initiative of his own device. He set into motion a multi-faceted scheme that involved setting up a pagan church organization modelled after that of the Christians. Maximinus empowered these provincial minions, the Hellenists, to act as his proxies in both disrupting Christian communities and harming Christians. He arranged it so that any written requests for action against the Christians originated with the local authorities and were addressed to the emperor. In so doing, he gave no indication to his fellow emperors of being in defiance of the law.

Maximinus Daia employed the indirect approach in renewing his campaign of persecution in 311. He quietly encouraged provincial authorities to make formal requests of him to deter the Christians from the practice of illegal religion. In one such letter from Arycanda, Lycia, dated about 312, the provincial authorities of Bishop Nicholas' home diocese of Lycia formally requested the emperor to assist them in their efforts to make the so-called atheists, the Christians, cease defying the observance of true piety, that is, state religion. The Lycians then went on in their letter to describe how they planned to forbid the Christians their detestable worship and to force them to practise the state religion.[56]

The perpetrators of violence against Christians eventually turned upon one another, igniting civil wars that flared up across the length and breadth of the Empire. In the cities of the Empire that ringed the Mediterranean Sea, the persecution that devastated the Christians became part of the warring among ambitious and desperate Roman commanders, which disrupted and threatened the lives of all the residents. Sea voyaging became treacherous due to attacks from naval forces. Under the pretext of military caution, the factional navies perpetrated outrages at sea that included boarding and piracy, destruction of ships, and the torture and murder of the voyagers. The heightened level of alarm and intense preparations for war agitated the residents of the seaports. They all feared, at any moment, a military attack that would visit horror and destruction upon them. Local workshops busily manufactured warships, naval weaponry and projectiles to equip the combatants for the next round of violence.[57]

As the persecution gained momentum in the years following the edict, it began to spin out of imperial control. What began as an attempt on the part of Diocletian to purify and strengthen the Empire became a bleeding wound that weakened it. Among the barbs of the edict was a measure that took away the Christians' right to a voice in the courts. This effectively blocked Christians from access to justice, so that charges against them would remain undisputed while they would have no recourse against injuries or false charges. This meant that predators could extort property, services or the last bronze coin from victims of the persecution by means of legal chicanery. A spiral of degeneration towards increased disorder and lawlessness quickly followed the very measures designed to reinforce the unity of the Empire.[58]

The social condition of the city of Rome during the fourth century was representative of the general degradation occurring in the Empire. One of the Empire's polished army officers from Antioch, Ammianus Marcellinus, apologized to any among his readers who were unfamiliar with the character of Rome that he wrote about—the "Eternal City" festering with riots, drunkenness and licentiousness. He wrote that, in spite of Rome's hard-won respect in the world, its majesty was tarnished by those among the high-born who revelled in vice and debauchery. Ammianus described Rome as a volatile city, too, with truculent crowds inciting civil disorder—for example, riots over the scarcity of wine or brawls over the outcome of chariot races.[59]

The declining condition of the Roman Empire that Augustus Diocletian had held so dear was reflected in microcosm in the course of his life and career after he launched the Great Persecution against the Christians. Diocletian, the author and orchestrator of the edict, was ironically one of its early casualties. After celebrating in Rome his twentieth year as caesar and anticipating his ninth consulship in the year 304, he escaped the tiresome crowd of libertines he had grown to despise and, in the cold of winter while suffering a respiratory illness, made a desperate overland journey to Nicomedia. For months, the Empire did not know if their principal augustus emperor was alive or dead. Then, on the Kalends (first) of March, Diocletian suddenly appeared in public, but prolonged illness had given him the pallor of death.

It was only a matter of days before Galerius, ravenous for the power Diocletian held, closed in on his adoptive father at Nicomedia to claim the purple robe of principal augustus. Galerius, full of ambition and confidence after his victory over the Persians, had already made secret preparations to seize the Empire. He had built up his army for a forced takeover should it prove necessary. He boldly announced to Diocletian that he was prepared to do by his own action what he requested of the ailing augustus. Breathing threats of civil chaos to the reluctant Diocletian, Galerius convinced the emperor to abdicate in the year 305. Thereby Diocletian, within two years of enacting his edict against the Christians, came to the end of his 20-year reign.[60]

Wasting little time, Galerius became augustus and, bypassing Constantius, whom he dared not unseat, immediately set his hand-picked top men in place, ready to begin ruling according to the basic principles of Diocletian's tetrarchy. The new tetrarchy in 306 emerged with Galerius as principal augustus in the East, Constantius as augustus in the West, and Severus and Maximinus Daia as subordinate caesars in the West and East respectively.

By the year 307, Galerius had ordered a new census to ascertain the taxable worth of citizens in the Empire. According to first-hand reports, he carried out the census brutally and clumsily. The immediate outcome was social disruption and confusion, such that additional census agents were dispatched to check on what their predecessors had done. The bungled census ultimately angered and alienated powerful families, especially in the city of Rome.

An eyewitness, Lactantius of Bithynia, gave an account of the census in which the census agents went everywhere and counted everything, treating the citizens as though they were captives. They measured fields parcel by parcel, counted vineyards and trees, recorded all kinds of animals and counted people. They brought everyone to the cities, gathering urban and rural people together. They filled the market squares with families and households, including children and slaves. The squares resounded with the cries of people suffering tortures and beatings from the authorities, who coerced the testimony of children against their parents, faithful slaves against their masters and wives against their husbands. When these investigations failed, people were tortured until they accused themselves of crimes they had not committed. The census takers made no allowance for age or health. They dragged out the sick and weak, estimating ages so that they added years to the young and subtracted them from the old. Such actions inflicted grief and sadness upon all.[61]

The citizens of the Empire came to see that they had more to hate about imperial authorities than Christian neighbours. Weary from years of chaos and civil war, they longed for just and able leadership and the peace and prosperity it would bring.

For a time, Galerius enjoyed the perception that all was proceeding in accordance with his will. Then one by one, the horses he used to propel the chariot of state began to elude his grasp.

Constantine slipped out of his control first. Galerius had passed him over for appointment to the tetrarchy. Galerius kept Constantine at the palace as a means to influence his father, Constantius, augustus emperor of the West. Constantius had repeatedly requested that Galerius send Constantine to him, and when Galerius half-heartedly signed a letter of permission—thinking he could change his mind later—Constantine unexpectedly and daringly fled to his father's side in Gaul. Constantius transferred his command over to Constantine, who then sent an announcement of his new status to Galerius. Against his will, Galerius invested Constantine with the purple robe of caesar. This he had to do, for he was in no position to deny Constantine that honour. This was a stinging blow to Galerius—in one stroke, he had lost control over the Augustus Emperor Constantius and a chance to choose his successor.[62]

Severus, one of Galerius' chosen men, became the next steed to disengage. Severus received a challenge to his authority from Maxentius in Rome, who, ironically, was son-in-law to Galerius. Maxentius had defied his father-in-law by using a revolt against the cruel census to catapult him to the office of caesar. Galerius, having no patience with Maxentius, authorized Severus to attack, and supplied him with an army to do so. Severus brought his army to the gates of Rome, where the soldiers promptly turned against him, tore down his standards and deserted him. Galerius stepped in, regained command of the army, executed Severus and brought the soldiers back to Rome, where they again balked at the formidable walls of their imperial capital. Galerius, then barely able to control the soldiers, set them loose on a destructive rampage across Italy on his way back home to Nicomedia. The citizens of Rome did not forget Galerius' barbarism.

The third troubled stallion reared up shortly after Galerius returned to the palace in Nicomedia from the debacle in Italy. Galerius sought the help of old Diocletian to rebuild the tetrarchy. Galerius planned to replace the ill-fated Severus with comrade-in-arms Licinius and to make his friend augustus of the East, an appointment he could make since Constantius' son Constantine held the rank of caesar. Galerius thus appointed Licinius to the second highest consulship of the Empire.

But Galerius could not have been prepared for what would follow. As soon as the news of Licinius reached Maximinus Daia's ears, his anger at not having been chosen as augustus turned to malevolence. Galerius learned of this and repeatedly sent delegations and letters urging him to yield his claim to the title of augustus. Ultimately, Galerius received an announcement from Maximinus that his army had proclaimed him augustus. Thus ended the comradeship between Galerius and Maximinus Daia.[63]

In March of 310, Galerius himself was unhorsed by an illness that would eventually prove fatal.

Maxentius had grown bold enough to assert claims on Constantine's domains. Constantine then moved against Maxentius at Rome. He deployed his army at Rome and arranged two flanks in the vicinity of the Milvian Bridge. Constantine had been inspired to mark the sign of the *chi rho* (☧), the first two Greek letters in the name of Christ, on his shields and standards. The battle began along two fronts.

Maxentius was hosting a circus within the walls of Rome to celebrate the fifth anniversary of his rule. His detractors among the crowd in the circus began to complain that he was deserting the public security. They openly shouted that Constantine could not be conquered. Maxentius hurried out of the circus and summoned the senators to consult the Sibylline Books, in which they found a prediction that, on this day, the enemy of the Romans would die. Maxentius was encouraged by the prophecy and went out with another force to join the battle.

Constantine's forces wedged Maxentius' troops against the Tiber River, so that their only route of escape was back across the Milvian Bridge. When Maxentius and his mass of fleeing troops rushed across the bridge, it collapsed. Maxentius and many members of his force drowned. Constantine then became senior augustus of the West.

Following the death of Galerius in April of 311, Maximinus Daia rose up, determined to prevail. He managed to bully his way past Licinius into Nicomedia. There he began to superimpose his own pagan clerical structure upon the whole of the East, to the effect that the pagan pontiffs and priests functioned and dressed like the Christian clerics. Maximinus issued instructions that the pagan clerics should sacrifice to the imperial deities, perform the pagan rituals, and actively persecute the Christians by preventing them from building churches and by bringing up charges against them in the courts.[64]

The condition of Asia Minor and the East under the reign of Maximinus Daia was fragile. Among those suffering the worst, Christians in Bishop Nicholas' diocese of Lycia struggled to survive while Nicholas was in prison and unable to help them. During the winter of 311 to 312, the rains failed and famine ensued. When the famine had taken hold, a new and malignant disease infected the people—an inflammation that covered the body with boils and attacked the eyes. People of all ages suffered with this disease, which blinded hundreds.

To add to this, the relentless Maximinus Daia made enemies of the Armenians by enforcing upon them the practice of the state religion of Rome. The Armenians rebelled, so the Emperor engaged them in war.

The people who lived in the cities of Asia Minor were so desperate for food that a measure of wheat, nine dry litres, cost as much as 2,500 Attic drachmas, more than the annual income of most people. In the small country towns and villages, so many people died from malnutrition and disease that the rural areas became depopulated. Those who had means were taken aback by the multitude of destitute people begging on the streets. For a while, the wealthier residents of the city gave to the poor, but they ceased giving when the thought occurred to the donors that, before long, they too would end up in a desperate situation. The bodies of the malnourished and sick who had died sometimes remained for days in the centres of the agorae.

In some instances, many of the wealthy—leaders, governors and officials—who could afford to buy food managed to escape the famine only to be struck down by the disease. The air was filled with cries of the grieving, and all that could be seen and heard in the roads, agorae and streets were processions of mourners playing the flute and beating their breasts.[65]

In the peak of troubles, pagans desperately sought relief. Cynicism and Pythagoreanism enjoyed popularity as two important philosophies, but they did not offer solace to an agitated pagan. Cynicism derived its content from the teachings of ancient Greek philosopher Antisthenes and, as a cult that shunned ease and pleasure, by definition offered no peace or comfort. Pythagoreanism, also a product of an ancient Greek thinker, Pythagoras, ascribed numerical descriptions to the universe and advocated a benevolent approach to life, but did not offer comfort to the stricken soul, although Pythagoras himself possibly believed in the transmigration of the soul. Roman imperial culture offered only three philosophical avenues by which a sensible pagan might escape from anguish—Epicurianism, Stoicism or Neoplatonism.

Epicurianism, from the ancient Greek philosopher Epicurus, taught that peace of mind represented the highest good, a person could attain good and endure evil, the soul was mortal and death negated feeling. Stoicism, founded by the early Greek thinker Zeno, informed its followers that they were actors in a cosmic play authored by the deities, that the limit of their freedom as actors was to decide how to play the part assigned to them, and that it was best for them to accept their lot in life. Neoplatonism, a third-century Roman adaptation of the philosophy of the ancient Greek master Plato, began where Plato left off—that is, it claimed that human beings could improve themselves, that their intellects excelled to the highest order and that they possessed souls. Neoplatonism attempted to describe how the individual soul could attain to God.[66]

Neoplatonism set itself apart from Epicurianism and Stoicism in that it offered the anguished pagan some hope of enduring the calamities of mortal life. Neoplatonism also presented the possibility of a path for one's soul to connect with God, which, to a pagan mind in the early fourth century, was a new concept. Neoplatonists made no bold promises to the converts—but the mystery religions, as well as Judaism and Christianity, did.

The so-called mystery religions on the one hand, with Judaism and Christianity on the other, carried farther both the hope of transcending mortal suffering and the concept of the soul uniting with God. The mystery religions included Mithraism and Orphism, the Bacchic and Eleusinian cults, and the worship of Isis and Cybele. These religions had in common a strong connection with nature and secret rites to initiate members and to celebrate the fertility, birth, death and rebirth of their gods and goddesses. The mystery religions existed in relative harmony with or as part of the official Roman state religion. By contrast, Judaism and Christianity stood outside the official religions of the Empire and required the faithful to worship one god in a prescribed way.[67]

Judaism was the first religion in the Roman Empire to prescribe the worship of one god according to one method and to the exclusion of any other deities. The Jews were able to maintain relative autonomy of religious practice in the imperial domains because they had set the legal pattern with Rome dating back to their alliance in the second century BCE. Early in their life within the Empire, the Jewish communities had adopted the practice of caring for the poor among them. Jewish community leaders, merchants, shopkeepers and others who earned at least a modest income made a regular practice of giving alms and furnishing employment to the needy of their faith. The unique Jewish practice of regularizing benevolence and cultivating solidarity within their congregations contrasted sharply with the high-profile and individualized gifts of wealthy pagan potentates to their splendid cities. In their practice, the strength of their communities and their evident attention to matters ethical and moral, the Jews drew many pagan converts to Judaism. Pagan converts could then receive God's dispensation to the Jews.

Christianity was the second religion in the Empire to establish the rigours of worshipping one god to the exclusion of any others. The Christians immediately aroused the disapproval and hostility of the Roman Empire and were on their guard against state persecutions throughout the Church's first three centuries. The Christian communities continued the Jewish practice of generosity towards the poor among them, and of providing alms and work opportunities for the needy of their faith.[68]

The Christian communities offered the anguished pagan a remedy for pains already suffered, the hope of transcending mortal suffering in the present and a promise of infinite joy in the eternal presence of God. Bishop Ignatius of Antioch urged his friend Polycarp, Bishop of Smyrna, to oversee his church with the wisdom of a serpent and the gentleness of a dove. He instructed Polycarp to speak with every worshipper and to bear their infirmities as his own. Ignatius charged Polycarp to seek out the more afflicted among the faithful, to determine their malaises and to apply therapeutic attentions to their remedies. He reminded Polycarp to take care of those who depended upon the Church for their physical survival. Lastly, Ignatius encouraged Polycarp to lead his people to God as a good captain conducts a ship to safe harbour—for, in so doing, he conducts them to eternal life.[69]

For other "captains" there would be no safe harbours. The avowed arch-enemy of the Christian God, Maximinus Daia, began a military gambit against Licinius that seemed to go well. He became bolder and, in the winter of 312 to 313, upon hearing that Licinius was involved with wedding celebrations in Milan in the company of his host Constantine, Maximinus took action. He moved his army—at great cost in losses due to harsh weather—from Syria across Asia Minor to the gates of Byzantium, a small Greek settlement. After an 11-day standoff with a small group of Licinius' rearguard, ample time for reports to be transmitted to Licinius, the guard capitulated to Maximinus and his army of 70,000. Maximinus then moved his forces to other small towns and was stalled in a similar manner for several days at each location.

These delays gave Licinius time to collect a force of about 30,000 and to take up an opposing position along the plain of Ergenus. The battle ensued on the morning of May 1, 313, with Licinius' soldiers gaining almost immediate domination over those of Maximinus. Within a short while, Maximinus saw about one-third of his force mowed down like hay before the scythe and another third surrendering; he and his family were among the last third, who made a hurried retreat east to Asia Minor.

With Licinius and his army in pursuit, Maximinus was able to elude capture by weaving through the Taurus mountain passes for only a few months, until what meagre good fortune he had clung to abandoned him. At Tarsus in September of 313, Maximinus was dead.[70]

The price paid by entire families and communities of Christians during Diocletian's Great Persecution of 303 to 313 has remained unknown. Some Christians survived these cruelties, others died at the hands of their persecutors. By the most reasonable accounts, the Great Persecution probably cost tens of thousands of Christians their freedom, and thousands of Christians their lives.[71]

CHAPTER 5

Bishop Nicholas in the New Era of Toleration

Constantine, now augustus emperor of the West, soon proved his affection for his Christian subjects by publishing, in June of 313, a circular letter that has become known as the "Edict of Milan," or "Edict of Toleration." It stated that toleration for Christianity was the new public policy. Speaking in the royal "we," Constantine reminded the imperial and provincial authorities that his court for some years had wished religious toleration for all, specifically, that Christians and non-Christians could freely practise their own religions. But, due to the conditions that Maximinus Daia had attached to the letter of toleration that the repentant Galerius had written from his deathbed in 311, Christians had been deterred from freely practising their faith.

Constantine announced that he and Licinius, the new augustus of the East, while together in Milan had decided the rules for reverencing the Deity, which called for Christians and all others to worship as they chose, in order that the heavenly powers would show favour to the emperors and the Empire. No one should be denied their right to be a Christian, and everyone could worship as need required, so that the Deity would bestow care and generosity upon all. Constantine and Licinius sent this letter to supersede and cancel the contrary conditions that accompanied the letter from Galerius, and to inform the deputy praetorian prefects in every region of the Empire that the emperors gave full permission for the Christians to practise their worship. All subjects of the Empire received the privilege to observe their own form of worship.

Constantine further ruled that all Christian places of meeting that had been confiscated from their corporate ownership under the persecution must be returned to the Christians without delay and without demand for compensation. Those non-Christian holders of Christian property who felt they had a legitimate claim could apply for compensation to the deputy praetorian prefect and magistrate of their region. Any other property the Christians as an organization had possessed before the persecution had to be restored to them without dispute. Again, those who suffered loss from this order who had a reasonable claim could request compensation of the aforementioned authorities.

Constantine emphasized that he expected his subordinates to carry out his orders quickly and energetically so that the public peace would be secured. By pressing the authorities into observance of this decree, Constantine hoped to ensure that the divine care that he perceived and had benefited from on previous occasions remained with the Empire forever. He ordered that the edict be published everywhere so that every citizen would be aware of his act of generosity.[72]

Finally, after 10 years and four months of state-sanctioned persecution, the torments abated. The pagans set aside their violence and allowed the Christians freedom and peace.

In Myra, Bishop Nicholas and the other surviving Christians were released from the prisons. Others who had been pressed into labour in the mines and quarries were released as well. Gradually, they made their way to the homes that served as hospices to care for the malnourished, sick, injured and dying victims of the persecution.

Soon after the new law of toleration had been published, the provincial magistrates returned to Christians properties that they had forcibly confiscated from them during the persecution. This provided more hospice beds to care for the casualties. Now Bishop

Nicholas and his presbyters were able to prepare and sanctify a place of worship.

Following the example set by the Apostles, Bishop Nicholas guided his diocese at Myra so faithfully that he became famous for his devotion to God, his advocacy of justice and his care for his people. After a long period of recovery and under the protection of law, the community of faithful gathered in their churches to celebrate liturgical services and feast days.

While Bishop Nicholas and Christians throughout the various regions of the Empire struggled to rebuild their communities, controversy flared and confronted Constantine with a bitter foretaste of the challenges he would face in trying to unify the Empire. In Carthage, a complex imbroglio developed, which came to be known as the "Donatist" controversy, although the problem actually began with Majorinus, who challenged the duly elected Bishop Caecilian. The anti-Caecilian faction had the backing of a unique Christian patroness named Lucilla. She allegedly fell out with the pro-Caecilian party because they scorned her for carrying around the bone of a martyr and kissing it before communion. In response, Lucilla provided generous financial backing to the opposing faction. Her funding of the effort resulted in the election of her hand-picked candidate, Majorinus. This resulted in Carthage having two bishops-elect: Caecilian and Majorinus. Another issue intensified the standoff—the pro-Caecilians were moderate if vocal in their acceptance of the *traditores*, while the pro-Majorinus clerics were hostile towards them.[73]

Constantine, with the support of Bishop Hosius of Cordoba, stepped into the fray determined to resolve this schism by an imperial commission at Rome composed of bishops who would hear the arguments from both sides. Interestingly, although he had appointed a council of bishops, Constantine kept the role of final judge for himself. Before the council convened in 313, Majorinus died and the pro-Majorinus faction replaced him with Donatus, from whom the label "Donatists" derived. The council voted in favour of Caecilian, proclaimed him innocent of charges levelled against him by the Donatists and recognized him as the duly elected Bishop of Carthage.

But the matter did not end there. The Donatists appealed the verdict of the council at Rome. Constantine accepted their appeal and convened a larger council of bishops to meet at Arles in 314. These bishops upheld the decision of the commission at Rome: Caecilian was innocent and entitled to be bishop.

Intoxicated with righteous indignation, the Donatists pressed the matter further by appealing to Constantine himself. What they had not counted on was that Constantine had taken the precaution of initiating a quiet inquiry in Africa into the Donatists' main charge against Caecilian—that he had been consecrated by a *traditor* named Felix, therefore his installation as bishop was invalid. Constantine's investigators uncovered an elaborate effort on the part of the Donatists to falsify evidence against the deceased Felix by adding a damning paragraph to one of his letters. Their master of illegal tactics was one Ingentius who, upon revealing this information to the chief investigator Aelianus, was promptly given a berth in the prison.[74]

To Constantine, the sight of Christian clergy exchanging charges and countercharges of *traditor* must have been an irritating display, but their tampering with evidence, forging of documents and attempts at legal entrapment against each other presented an especially ugly spectacle of factionalism that hinted at ingratitude before God. In the many twists and turns that the struggle with the Donatists took, Constantine edged closer and closer to the precipice of violence against Christians for whom he had come to believe himself the chosen protector.

Yet, even as the pot simmered in Carthage, another had begun to boil in Asia Minor. Licinius originally had become augustus by order of his old army friend Galerius. Even though Licinius had married Constantine's half-sister Constantia and had co-signed the Edict of Milan, he did not embrace Constantine's vision of an Empire that tolerated all faiths. Rather, Licinius held to the pagan course of restoration. After a series of misunderstandings and open hostilities between the two augusti, Licinius adopted a policy of harassment and violence against the Christians in his provinces in the East.

This emboldened the Hellenists once again to inflict damage and injury upon the Christians, just as they were rebuilding their lives and communities from the devastations of the Great Persecution. Bishop Nicholas with his presbyteras and presbyters, deaconesses and deacons, were again on the defensive against renewed cruelties from their Hellenist neighbours, who were still indignant after being thwarted at the hands of Augustus Constantine.

Constantine realized that he would have to confront Licinius. The effort needed to dominate Licinius presented a formidable challenge. Constantine set to work building up his forces. Under his personal command, he assembled a versatile army of 120,000, composed of his more seasoned veterans from the barbarian frontiers of the West. He also placed his son Crispus in command of a hastily gathered fighting fleet of 200 light war galleys and a supply fleet of 2,000 merchant ships.

Licinius commanded 150,000 troops and 15,000 cavalry, and his naval fleet arrayed 350 warships, which he placed in the hands of his admiral Abantus. Licinius set up his stronghold at Hadrianople on the European side of the Propontis, from which he could sweep across the West after he had defeated Constantine.

Constantine attacked from Thessalonica and clashed with Licinius on July 3, 324. The armies of both sides incurred heavy casualties, but Licinius turned east and refortified at Byzantium with his back to the Bosphorus strait and the Propontis. Constantine followed and laid siege to the fortress. However, Licinius was able to hold fast for almost three months because he could supply his troops from his ships on the seaside of Byzantium. Constantine then boldly sent Crispus and his small fleet to engage the superior fleet of Licinius.

Crispus must have learned his Greek history well: just as the ancient Greek commander Themistocles during the Medic Wars in 480 BCE had defeated a superior naval force, Crispus somehow arranged his 200 light galleys so that Abantus and the captains of his 350 warships found themselves tightly bottled up in the Propontis. Thus Crispus was able to breach Abantus' ships at will, sinking 130 of them and delivering a decisive defeat to Licinius' navy.

Licinius fled Byzantium and retreated east across the Bosphorus to Asia Minor. He prepared to defend his home territory and had gathered many more troops for the purpose. He made his stand at Chrysopolis. On September 18, Constantine fought a second great battle with Licinius. When the din of battle had subsided, Constantine and his army, who campaigned under the banner of the *chi rho*, had carried the day.

Licinius returned to his palace in Nicomedia and played his last card; he prevailed upon Constantia to plead his case before her half-brother Constantine. This seemed to work, as Licinius presented himself at court and, for a time, found Constantine to be a gracious host. Some time after his removal to Thessalonica, however, Licinius met his end.[75]

Thus Constantine had defeated Licinius, augustus emperor of the East, last of the tetrarchs appointed by Galerius. Finally, as sole emperor of all Rome, Constantine was prepared to consolidate his power. Aware of the unstable condition of the Western Empire and responsive to an ancestral yearning for ancient Greece, Constantine began constructing a new capital on the site of the Greek settlement of Byzantium.

Under the protection of Constantine the Great, Christianity began its rise to tentative, then stable footing among the faiths in the Empire. In Myra, Bishop Nicholas had restored his community to their devotions of worship. Yet, even in peace, overwhelming challenges lay ahead. The joy and profound relief the Christians felt at having survived, at having thrown off the chains of their tormentors, could not erase the deep scars inflicted upon them during the years of destruction and suffering.

It was approaching harvest time in Lycia, and the Androkos River diminished and calmed, just as it had in the dry heat of late summer in many years past. But what was there for the Christians to harvest this year? Under the emperors Maximinus Daia and Licinius, the countryside had been all but depopulated. The few farmers who had survived the wars had not produced enough food to support the residents of Myra.

A Greek story tells about the famine in Lycia and how Bishop Nicholas helped feed his people. In Lycia, the land was barren and a famine ensued. Bishop Nicholas took it upon himself to rescue his diocese from starvation. Merchant ships filled with grain came to anchor in the harbour near Myra on their way to Constantinople. Bishop Nicholas entreated the ships' captains to deposit some of the produce at Myra. The captains refused at first, but Bishop Nicholas prevailed. The captains unloaded hundreds of measures of grain, and thus did Bishop Nicholas save Myra from starvation. The people of Myra praised God for rescuing them.[76]

Bishop Nicholas and the survivors of the 10 years of persecution bore the scars of grief. The Christians grieved for those they had lost and for those who had suffered at the hands of their tormentors. A few of the perpetrators still lived among their neighbours. A large number of survivors experienced their pain as rage, and a minority of angry Christians retaliated against their non-Christian neighbours, destroying pagan shrines and temples, and defacing Hellenistic and Roman statuary.

The Christians who made their way to Myra included those who had escaped the fury of the persecution. Some had gone into hiding in the mountains and caves, and others had moved to more tolerant lands. But there was yet another group, those who had co-operated with the authorities in order to save themselves. These were the *traditores*, Christians who had surrendered holy books or church furnishings, and *thurificatores*, Christians who had sacrificed to the imperial deities.[77]

While the Christians returning from abroad and from hiding places in the mountains and caves happily resumed communion with the churches, the traditores and thurificatores presented Bishop Nicholas and his presbyters with a terrible quandary. How could they bring those people who had turned away from Christ back into communion?

Fortunately, Bishop Nicholas could look to the examples set by other bishops who had faced this problem before him. One such example, from the third century, was Bishop Gregory of Neo-Caesarea in Asia Minor. In his *Canonical Epistle*, Bishop Gregory listed the misdeeds carried out by Christians during a barbarian invasion and occupation in the years 260 to 267. He set forth the penances required to restore those who could be brought back into communion.[78]

Bishop Nicholas, the priests, deaconesses and deacons, overcame their own frailty and provided strength and encouragement to those around them. The work of tending to the sick and rebuilding their community helped to unify and strengthen the faithful. The examples of the Apostles and the post-apostolic leaders of the Church inspired them in their service.

In 325, a matter of grave importance had to be resolved before Constantine could bring to fruition his new vision of a *Pax Romana* founded upon God-inspired leadership and unity by virtue of justice and religious tolerance. Constantine viewed with alarm the heightened tenor of debate among Christians over matters of doctrine.

Constantine expressed his deep agitation in his letter to the chief opponents in the latest dispute: Alexander, Bishop of Alexandria, and Arius, a priest of that city. In his letter, Constantine characterized the dispute as one that began when Alexander questioned each of his presbyters on his view of a piece of insignificant text from the Law, and Arius answered flippantly, giving an ill-conceived and worthless opinion. Constantine's letter continued with his observation that, once this dispute occurred, Alexander and Arius abandoned fellowship and divided the Christian community. Constantine, who referred to himself as their fellow servant, urged them to pardon each other equally.[79]

When Alexander and Arius refused to make peace, Constantine called for a general assembly of the bishops to be held at Nicaea. He hosted the bishops himself. Constantine personally presided over the council meetings, which were reported by Eusebius of Caesarea.

The council to resolve the dispute convened in the largest hall within the palace. Tiered seating lined the walls. The clerics entered and took their assigned seats. When the bishops and other invitees to the council had seated themselves, they grew quiet in anticipation of the emperor's entrance. The emperor's inner circle of friends entered the hall one by one and formed two lines to either

D.L. Cann

Along a rim of hills were the unmistakable grey, hand-cut stone buildings of the ancient port, Andriacus.

D.L. Cann

The courtyard of Myra's amphitheatre was littered with huge stone blocks that were probably part of the gate and stage structures.

D.L. Cann

The amphitheatre at Myra had felt presence, as if the distance of 1700 years between our time and theirs was but a thin veil.

D.L. Cann

The exterior of the recently excavated sixth-century Church of Saint Nicholas in Myra. In the distance, we can see the rugged Taurus Mountains.

D.L. Cann

From the west entrance, into the narthex of the Church of Saint Nicholas streamed the rose and gold rays of the setting sun. They cast an amber light upon the apsis and synthronon, illuminating the six columns that stood about the altar so they appeared to glow like lamps.

D.L. Cann

Looking out from the Church of Saint Nicholas toward the colonnade. This was probably a former market in the early fourth century that opened onto the Androkos River.

Icon of Saint Nicholas of Myra *in the collection of the Antalya Museum. Ministry of Culture, Republic of Turkey.*

Key centres in Christianity at the time of Saint Nicholas

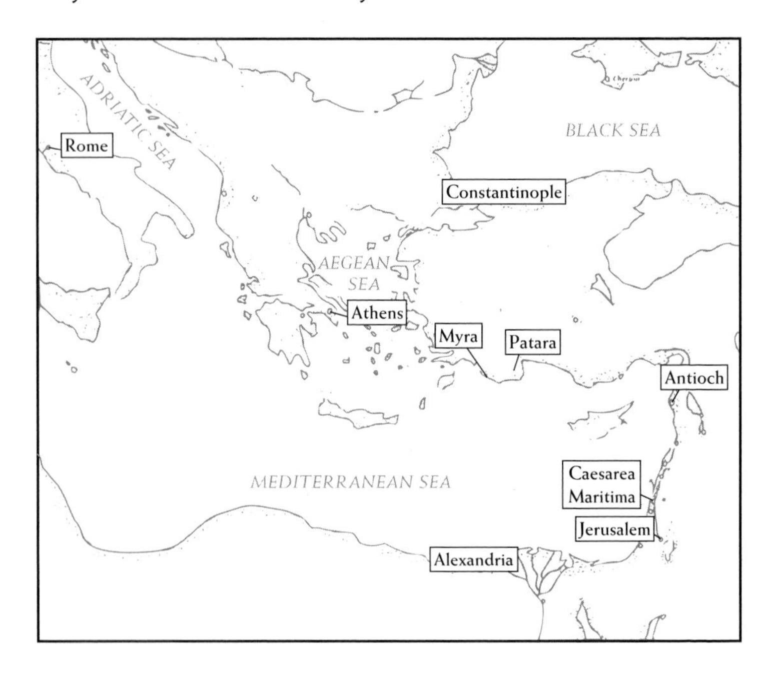

side. A signal alerted the approach of the emperor and everyone stood up. The Emperor Constantine entered the hall between the rows of his friends. He was adorned like a messenger from heaven—from his light-coloured mantle to the sheen of his purple robe, and the rainbow sparkles of light reflected in the gold and gems that studded his garments—and his physical appearance was matched by his imperial bearing. When Constantine had advanced to the end of the tiers of seats to a small gilded chair, he first nodded to the bishops, who returned his acknowledgment, and then sat down. The entire gathering of the council took their seats also.

The bishop seated immediately at Constantine's right side stood to deliver a poetical speech, offering a hymn of gratitude to God for their beloved emperor. In the silence that followed, all eyes rested on the emperor. Constantine regarded those assembled before him, and then began to speak in Latin with a Greek interpreter.

Constantine told the assembly that he had prayed that he might enjoy the company of the bishops and clerics, and God had granted it. He was grateful to the Ruler because, along with all the other blessings, God had given a special one, which was for Constantine to receive all of those in the assembly and to find them sharing the same faith. The emperor warned the clergy not to allow an enemy to destroy their peace; now that he had defeated the tyrants against God by the saving grace of God, he could not bear to see another enemy capture their faith by deceit. The augustus warned the bishops that the division threatening the Church was more dangerous than any battle, and could cause more pain than they would face in combat. Constantine shared his dismay that, when he, with Supreme help, had defeated their enemies he had thought he could then celebrate with all who were free from their tyranny. On the contrary, he heard of the dispute threatening the Church and immediately sent for them to seek a resolution. Constantine was happy that the clerics had gathered there and he anticipated that they would soon be in communion and that, as ministers of God, they would announce their harmony to all. He charged them to hasten to resolve the dispute among them that they might be freed from the constraints of division and return to the rule of peace. Constantine assured them that in so doing they would please God and give happiness to their fellow servant.

After Constantine had delivered his address, he opened discussion to the council. Some bishops launched accusations against their neighbours, who, in turn, responded with countercharges. Each side voiced numerous proposals and much controversy ensued. The emperor listened to the speakers patiently and gently guided the disputants towards mutual understanding.[80]

Constantine shocked many delegates from the East by suggesting that Eusebius insert the phrase "of one substance with the Father" to describe the nature of the Son. Eusebius of Caesarea obeyed, in spite of the fact that in 268 the Council of Antioch had condemned the phrase. The bishops responded with overwhelming agreement, with the exception of Secundus of Ptolemais and Theona of Marmirice, who were Libyan countrymen of Arius. These two men, along with Arius and his followers, as well as Eusebius of Nicomedia and Theognis of Nicaea, all found themselves excommunicated until they could come to agreement with the new proclamation of faith known as the Nicene Creed. These holdouts eventually did come to some form of rapprochement when Constantine reconvened the Council of Nicaea later that year.[81]

When their work was completed, Constantine honoured the bishops with a state dinner at his palace, described by Eusebius of Caesarea. The twentieth year of Constantine's rule coincided with the completion of the council. The emperor honoured the ministers of God at a state banquet, which all the clerics attended. The event defied description. Palace guards stood with swords drawn in formation at the doors. The guests passed the guards and entered the rooms of the imperial household. They reclined at table on couches, some with Constantine and others to either side. The emperor's hospitality was outstanding, and he offered gifts to each of the guests.[82]

Eusebius of Caesarea recorded that bishops had come together from all the churches that filled the Empire. The status of Myra as the capital of the province of Lycia in Asia Minor supports the probability that Bishop Nicholas received an invitation to the council. There is evidence that Bishop Nicholas attended the Council of Nicaea—a document dated 510 lists Nicholas as a participant. The Greek tradition, however, is mixed on whether Bishop Nicholas attended. The hagiographers agree that Bishop Nicholas guided the souls in his care to faith in the gospel of Christ. By that description, Bishop Nicholas would have advocated against a doctrine that contradicted the scriptural teachings of Christ.[83]

The Christian bishops received unexpected support from the imperial government in their efforts to rebuild the churches. Constantine's largesse to the Church included gifts of funds and authorization of judicial powers to the bishops. Suddenly, the bishops were given the power to grant Roman citizenship and render final judgments in cases of justice.[84]

Greek tradition tells of Nicholas intervening to save victims of false prosecution. In Myra, the relatives and friends of victims of injustice certainly would have sought the help of Bishop Nicholas, and would have appealed to him for final judicial remedy. In one incident described in the Greek tradition, residents of Myra called upon Bishop Nicholas, who was accompanied by visiting Roman commanders, to intercede on behalf of three innocents who had been wrongly accused and sentenced to death. The residents claimed that the magistrate had rendered judgment after receiving a bribe. Nicholas rushed to the place where the innocents awaited execution. He commanded the executioner to stop, released the innocents and confronted the magistrate with a charge of bribery to which he confessed.[85]

Constantine published the outcome of the Council of Nicaea to all the clergy in a series of letters to the provinces. His words for the Jews were less charitable than his efforts towards their communities. While he wrote harshly about them in his first post-Nicaea letter, in policy he showed more kindness by allowing the Jewish clergy to be legally exempt from obligatory, and often most onerous, administrative service to the Empire.[86]

What emerged was more than a period of peace. The Roman Empire under Constantine has been likened to a reflection of the kingdom in heaven. In this earthly model of the heavenly kingdom, the ruler was in a special relationship with God and the subjects prospered in the glory of a nation that enjoyed the protection of God.[87]

By 330, Constantine's architects and artisans had masterfully built Constantinople, also known as New Rome, upon the triangle of land that bordered the Bosphorus and the Propontis, and that guarded the nexus of trade routes across land and sea for West and East. Thus began the so-called Byzantine Empire and the great Period of Christian Recognition.

Constantinople, by fourth-century standards, was a magnificent city. For the new capital of the Empire, Constantine's architects created grand buildings, palaces, markets, hippodromes and churches. The gleaming capital, skirted with great walls, proudly commanded a prominence above the strait. According to an eyewitness, the emperor adorned his new capital with many churches, shrines to martyrs and grand residences. He dedicated the city to God and discouraged idol worship. In the city squares, he constructed fountains and decorated them with images of the Good Shepherd. In other sites, he placed sculptures, such as Daniel and the lions, cast in bronze and gilded with gold leaf. The emperor was so inspired that, in the royal apartments of the palace, he installed a chapel featuring a crucifix inset with gold and precious stones.[88]

The population of the grand city quickly grew, perhaps to a hundred thousand during Constantine's reign. And what a colourful place it must have been—narrow streets busy with activity and commerce, crowded with people from all corners of the Empire clad in every type, texture and colour of costume, from gold-embroidered scarlet and indigo robes of silk to trim imperial uniforms fitted out with glittering emblems and full regalia; the myriad aromas of food, spices, beverages and animals; and an exotic chorus of voices, the lilting music of reeds, flutes and strings, along with the percussive rhythms of feet, bangles, hooves, tack, wheels and drums.

There was special cause for Christians in the Eastern Roman Empire to celebrate with a joyful noise. Bishop Nicholas, who had tasted the full bitterness of the Great Persecution had seen enough goodwill from Emperor

Constantine to trust that the new peace between the Hellenists and the Christians would last. Bishop Nicholas had triumphed against the violence of the persecutors. By his prayers and pastoral care, he had guarded the souls of the Christians in his diocese of Lycia; by his support to those in need, he had contributed to the survival and renewal of families; by his courageous stand against the persecutors, he had shielded threatened children and families; and by advocating on behalf of the innocent, he had upheld justice.

Chapter 6

The Legacy of Saint Nicholas

Greek stories and first-hand historical accounts of life in the third- and fourth-century Eastern Roman Empire have helped us to picture the original Saint Nicholas. If we had encountered Bishop Nicholas at his church in Myra in, for example, the year 325, we would have found ourselves in the presence of a great soul who loved God wholeheartedly, who had chosen to endure years in a provincial Roman prison as a witness to his faith. We would have seen how he loved dearly the people of his community, and took up his vocation in order to share the joys and hope that God offers to all who seek the divine. In our visit with Bishop Nicholas, we would have seen him serving the people of Patara and Myra, quietly providing generous gifts to contribute to the survival and renewal of people and their families. We would have experienced Saint Nicholas as a person who gave freely of his kindness, wisdom, strength and spiritual vision to care for the souls and lives of his people during the harsh years in conflict with the Hellenists and in the brighter years of the New Rome under the benevolent Emperor Constantine I.

Let us look back to the late third century to follow the life and legacy of Saint Nicholas of Myra. Nicholas was born in about the year 275 in Patara, Lycia, on the Mediterranean coast of Asia Minor. He grew up in a town that shared in the imperial culture of the Roman Empire, but retained the Greek language and Hellenistic culture of the East. Nicholas' family worked among Christian trades and craftspeople and brought him up in the way of the faith and in communion with the Church. The generation of Nicholas' parents remembered the time when the Emperor Valerian had turned against his Christian subjects, calling upon his provincial magistrates and their Hellenist friends in the East to persecute the churches and their leaders. This made Nicholas' parents and the other Christian adults in their community especially protective towards each other and their children.

As Nicholas grew, his parents nurtured him in his faith, and encouraged him in his decision to become a priest. In his study of the Scriptures and of the Christian forerunners, Nicholas learned the beliefs and practice of his faith. The Greek tradition informs us that, during his young adulthood, Nicholas put his faith into practice when he secretly donated purses of coins to a poor family who were on the point of selling their children into slavery. His gifts of money to this family saved them from destruction.

From his youth, Nicholas prepared himself—first with the Greek disciplines of grammar, rhetoric and philosophy, followed by the rich, Christian literary tradition that included the Septuagint Old Testament, the Gospels and the Letters and the writings of the post-apostolic authors—to become the exemplary servant of God we know him to have been. The original stories of his life tell us that, as a priest, Nicholas demonstrated the qualities that Polycarp had illustrated in his second-century letter to the Philippians. Priest Nicholas showed a great capacity for sympathy, compassion towards humankind and concern for reclaiming those who had become lost and alienated, or were ill. He provided help to widows, orphans and others in need. Priest Nicholas conducted himself in a way that was honourable before God and people. He restrained himself from anger, favour or unfairness, and did not seek to acquire money. Priest Nicholas, aware that none are without fault, refrained from judging and criticizing others. He forgave others their misdeeds before seeking to have God forgive his, believing that all live under God's economy and Christ's judgment. Priest Nicholas served the Church with the awe and reverence exemplified by Jesus Christ, the Apostles and the Prophets.

We have limited information about events in Nicholas' life as a priest. We can make an informed guess that he became a priest while in his early twenties and served as a priest in Patara for a few years before he moved to Myra. We know that people of all types travelled frequently and over long distances in the Empire so it is possible that Nicholas could have travelled to Jerusalem, then known by its Roman name as Aelia Capitolina. If Nicholas did travel to Jerusalem, he would have prayed at the sites along the walk of Christ.

Nicholas served as a priest in Patara for perhaps as long as seven years. News probably came to him that the church at Myra needed help. It is even possible that his elder priest or a bishop directed him to go and serve at Myra. In any event, Nicholas decided to make the trip to Myra in order to serve as a priest in the church there.

By the time Priest Nicholas undertook the journey to Myra, the Great Persecution under Emperor Diocletian had begun in the East and both Patara and Myra were under the enforcement of Diocletian's edict against the Christians. In both cities, the atmosphere for Christians would have been something like a forced occupation by a hostile militia. Christians were keeping to themselves, while accusers, vigilantes and usurpers sought their next victims.

Arriving to begin his priestly service, Nicholas found Myra to be a dangerous and stricken city. Within a short while, Myra's bishop passed away, leaving the episcopal see vacant. In the early fourth century, the procedure for selecting a bishop in the larger cities had begun to shift from the local presbyters making a choice to an influential regional bishop making a nomination with the support of other bishops. The Greek tradition presents the selection of Nicholas as Bishop of Myra according to both procedures. Even though it was the capital of the province of Lycia, with a population of about 50,000, Myra was a city of secondary importance. By contrast, Antioch, one of the Eastern Roman Empire's major cities, had a population approaching 200,000. Since Myra was of more provincial than imperial significance, it is most likely that the presbyters at Myra selected their new bishop themselves. Let us assume that the presbyters selected Nicholas on his merits after having observed his devotion as one of their priests.

Nicholas was about 30 years of age when he became Bishop of Myra. At the time of his appointment, around 305, Diocletian's persecution of the Christians raged furiously in the East. It is probable that Nicholas was arrested by magistrates soon after he became Bishop of Myra.

Bishop Nicholas faced a desperate struggle at Myra when he was imprisoned for his faith under the Great Persecution. Under Diocletian's edict, the church at Myra was probably destroyed along with its sacred books. Bishop Nicholas had been prepared for conflict with the Hellenists, and he drew upon the skills that he had learned from his youth in the Christian community at Patara to peacefully resist their assaults and to protect his community of Christians. He would have suffered imprisonment first, then, at intervals, the magistrates would have tried to force him, along with the other Christian prisoners, to make sacrifice to the state deities. When he refused, Nicholas would have been beaten or tortured and thrown back into prison.

Confined to prison, Nicholas must have felt deep sorrow that he could not minister to his parish and diocese. As bishop, he was the guardian of the souls in his parish and diocese, and must have longed to be among his people to protect and guide them.

To emerge, triumphant, from such torment and mistreatment was perhaps the greatest victory for Bishop Nicholas. His endurance of several years imprisonment was testimony to his faith in Christ, and he would have seen this victory as one for all Christians in his diocese, and not just for himself. After his release, and that of his fellow Christian prisoners, probably around late summer of 313, Bishop Nicholas witnessed the unfolding of a most improbable sequence of events. The Hellenists were toppling from the height of power and meeting destruction at the hands of Emperor Constantine; sympathetic to the Christians, Emperor Constantine ordered freedom, toleration and restoration for his Christian subjects throughout the Roman world. Constantine proceeded to make gifts to the Church, and to empower the bishops with final judicial authority in civil and criminal cases in their towns and cities.

Returning to preside over the church in Myra after his release from prison would have been a bittersweet experience for Bishop Nicholas. He must have felt great joy as he was reunited with his parish, and at the same time, sorrow, as he acknowledged the number of people who were sick or injured, or had been lost from the community.

The survivors of the 10 years of persecution grieved for those they had lost and for those who had suffered at the hands of their tormentors. A few of the perpetrators lived among them, and a number of enraged Christians retaliated against their non-Christian neighbours, violating the principle of forgiveness that Bishop Nicholas had been taught by the Gospels and the Letters of the Apostles, as well as by Polycarp, a post-apostolic leader.

In the disastrous wake of the emperors Maximinus Daia and Licinius, there were few people left in the villages and countryside of Asia Minor. The working farms that remained after the wars had not produced enough food to prevent famine in the province of Lycia. A Greek story tells how Bishop Nicholas helped feed the people of his diocese by diverting grain to Myra from grain ships bound for the West. The original story, with the Latin title *Praxis de navibus frumentariis in portu,* comes to us from Michael the Archimandrite, who wrote it in Greek during either the late eighth or early ninth century. The story begins with a famine in Lycia. Bishop Nicholas desperately sought grain for the starving people of his diocese. Grain ships put into harbour at Myra's port of Andriaki on their voyage from Alexandria, Egypt, to Constantinople, the new capital of the Roman Empire. Bishop Nicholas met with the ships' captains and entreated them to release some of their produce to feed the famine-stricken people of Lycia. The captains refused at first, fearing that they would be held to account in Constantinople for any loss of their cargo. Bishop Nicholas persevered, however, assuring the captains that they would not suffer any adverse judgment. He persuaded them to unload hundreds of measures of grain. Bishop Nicholas distributed the grain, which nourished the hungry of Lycia for two years and provided them with seed to plant and harvest.[89]

When Bishop Nicholas passed away in the first half of the fourth century, his parish laid him to rest in Myra. Two hundred years after their beloved bishop died, Christians of Myra moved the body, or relics, of Saint Nicholas to another resting place in a small, sixth-century basilica that the people of Myra built and named in his honour.

With the conclusion of his life on earth, Saint Nicholas continued to live in the hearts of his devotees through his saintly legacy. Saint Nicholas of Myra has come to be venerated as the patron of many types of people—sailors, children, even convicted criminals, to name a few. The first saintly patronage attributed to Bishop Nicholas occurred in the East. Christians of the East called upon Saint Nicholas as the protector of victims of injustice.

The earliest story to bring fame to Saint Nicholas of Myra was *Protection of the Innocents*.

> People ran to Bishop Nicholas from the city of Myra crying, "Master, had you been present in the city, the magistrate would not have condemned three innocents to execution. We are in despair because we could not find Your Holiness!" Upon hearing this news, Holy Nicholas ran to where a crowd had gathered around the place of execution. The executioner held his sword up, waiting for the bishop. When Bishop Nicholas arrived, he found the executioner standing over the three innocents who were bound, kneeling and awaiting their deaths. Immediately, Holy Nicholas boldly snatched the sword from the executioner and threw it to the ground. He released the innocents and took them with him to the city. Then Bishop Nicholas burst into the chambers of the magistrate, Eustathius. The magistrate approached to give him honour, but Nicholas spurned him saying, "Evil murderer! How do you dare greet me, caught up as you are in so many evil deeds! I will inform Emperor Constantine about your treachery and the manner in which you govern the region he has entrusted to you." Hearing this, Eustathius bent to his knees and pleaded to the

> bishop, "Please do not lay this charge upon me, sir; the truth is I am not guilty, for it was the wish of my masters Eudoxius and Simonides." Ignoring his plea, Holy Nicholas retorted, "Eudoxius and Simonides did not cause this evil; it was silver and gold." Bishop Nicholas said this because he had learned that the magistrate expected a bribe of over two hundred pounds to falsely accuse and execute these citizens. Holy Nicholas did pardon the magistrate, after hearing pleas on his behalf from officers of the army and after Eustathius cleared the innocent citizens of his false accusations.[90]

Almost immediately, *Protection of the Innocents* began to be enhanced in the telling so that, by the fifth century, it had probably become a two-part tale, with each story featuring the same essential figures. In both stories, the victims of injustice face imminent destruction until Bishop Nicholas intervenes as the champion of justice to rescue them.

The differences between the two stories are significant. In the first, the setting is Myra, where townspeople plead with Bishop Nicholas to prevent the unjust execution of innocent people. He hastens to the victims, sets them free and confronts the magistrate with a charge of injustice prompted by greed. The second story, which we refer to as *Three Generals*, is the one more recently associated with Bishop Nicholas of Myra. *Three Generals* moves the setting to Constantinople and a later date, where Roman generals who have been unjustly condemned pray to God for their rescue and invoke the name of Bishop Nicholas. Though Nicholas remains physically in Myra, the story incorporates the assertion that he appears to the emperor and his prefect in Constantinople in their dreams, and persuades them to release the innocent generals. Essentially, the story of *Three Generals* appears to be a mirror image of *Protection of the Innocents,* with more colourful and heroic flourishes.

Both these stories were appreciated by medieval Eastern Romans. In the political and social tumult of the Eastern Roman Empire—where rulers of the imperial government and prelates of the Church were made and unmade at the stroke of pen or sword, and the common people suffered one catastrophe after another—it was comforting to have as champion Saint Nicholas, the saint who would stand up against perpetrators of injustice and secure victory for his people. His name in Greek, *Nikolaos*, means "victor for people." For the medieval Eastern Romans, Saint Nicholas had become a champion of justice working for the common people.

For those under the rule of Constantinople, the struggle between the temporal and heavenly realms was keenly felt. From the reign of Constantine I in the early fourth century, "caesaro-papism," or the primacy of the supreme leader in both secular and church affairs, became the ruling model for the next 10 centuries in the Eastern Roman Empire. The East was the setting for a vigorous, even apocalyptic, struggle between the kingdoms of earth and heaven. Despite the new and more tolerant Roman Empire, justice for the common people remained elusive.

Let us look at the East during the reign of Constantius II, a son of Constantine and Fausta, in the middle decades of the fourth century. Ammianus Marcellinus provides us with a contemporary view of life in the East under the Praetorian Prefect Musonian. Distinguishing himself by his linguistic skills in Latin and Greek, Musonian first rose to prominence when Constantine I employed him in his investigations of the Manichaean sect. The Manichaeans followed the teachings of Mani, who promoted a dualistic cosmic order and thus challenged the supremacy of the Godhead. Later in his career as praetorian prefect of the East under Constantius II, Musonian ruled discreetly and wisely except when the opportunity for gain presented itself. His conduct in the judicial proceedings following the mob killing of Theophilus, governor of Syria, resulted in several innocent people being condemned, while the wealthy perpetrators of the crime bought their release by the transfer of wealth and property to Musonian. While Musonian and his cronies in the military grew wealthy at the expense of their own subjects, the frontiers routinely suffered destructive raids by hostile neighbouring forces.[91]

Under such harsh conditions, the popularity and saintly patronage of Bishop Nicholas developed rapidly. The first surviving collection of Saint Nicholas legends originated in Constantinople, where Michael the

Archimandrite gathered a series of Nicholas stories to make into a biography, which was based upon the spoken tradition centred at Myra. The author may have published his work as early as the late eighth century, for it is known to have existed in the early ninth century. Michael the Archimandrite's *Bios* of Saint Nicholas of Myra included five tales in Greek. Their titles follow in both Latin and Greek.[92]

1. *Praxis de tribus filiabus/Praxeon pros tautas treis thiyateras.* Young Nicholas learns that a family is destitute, and the parents plan to sell their children into slavery. Nicholas secretly delivers money to the family in order to save them from ruin.
2. *Praxis de innocentes, Praxis de stratelatis/Praxeon pros tous treis stratelatas.* In *Praxis de innocentes,* Saint Nicholas learns that three innocent citizens are about to be executed. He hurries to rescue them, and then confronts the offending magistrate with a charge of injustice due to bribery. In *Praxis de stratelatis,* three innocent generals have been unjustly accused of treason and are sentenced to execution. They pray to God for their rescue, invoking the spirit of Bishop Nicholas of Myra in their prayers. The innocent are released after the emperor and his praetorian prefect are visited by Bishop Nicholas, who demands that justice prevail.
3. *Praxis de nautis/Praxeon pros tous nautai.* Mariners at sea become grounded in a severe storm. They pray to God for their rescue, calling upon the spirit of Bishop

Nicholas of Myra. The mariners free their ship from imminent destruction and sail to Myra to thank Bishop Nicholas, whom they credit with rescuing them.

4. *Praxis de navibus frumentariis in portu/ Praxeon pros ploiou.* A famine has taken hold in Lycia, threatening the whole province, including Myra, with starvation. Bishop Nicholas diverts grain from visiting ships and distributes it to save the people of Myra.
5. *Thauma de Artemide/Thauma pros tes Artemis.* Saint Nicholas warns pilgrims who are en route to visit his church in Myra to dispose of the evil balm they have unwittingly accepted from Artemis.

One story, *Praxis de nautis*, from Michael the Archimandrite's *Life* of Saint Nicholas, takes place in the eastern Mediterranean. A ship is driven by a gale during a severe storm and runs aground. Caught on the shoals, the ship and its company are in grave danger of being destroyed, as wind and waves batter the ship against the rocks. The captain and crew, having heard of Bishop Nicholas as a holy servant of God, invoke the spirit of Nicholas of Myra at the same time as they pray to God for rescue. The sailors claim to receive help from Bishop Nicholas himself, who appears to the crew and encourages them to reinforce the masts and to free the ship from the rocks. They then sail to Myra, where they visit Bishop Nicholas at his church and thank him for his help in their rescue.

Michael the Archimandrite gives us the earliest written story of *Praxis de nautis* that has survived, though historical texts offer tantalizing hints that earlier written biographies of Saint Nicholas of Myra existed. *Praxis de nautis* comes to us in the earliest decades of the ninth century—500 years after the death of Bishop Nicholas of Myra. The author based his story upon the spoken tradition of the region around Myra, writing it a hundred years before Symeon Logotheta, or Symeon Metaphrastes, "the Translator," appropriated the fanciful and confused stories that appear in his biography of Saint Nicholas. Michael the Archimandrite's *Praxis de nautis* is more reliable than the sea rescues related by Symeon and other hagiographers because it was written nearer the time the original spoken story was recorded and it is free from confusion with another Lycian saint, Nicholas of Sion, from the fifth century.

The stories Michael the Archimandrite gathered in his biography of Saint Nicholas represent the spoken legends of the day. As such, these are the earliest known stories about the life of Nicholas. These original Saint Nicholas stories inspired Joseph the Hymnograph and Theodorus the Studite to pen, in the early ninth century, what may be the oldest hymn to honour our saint. Michael the Archimandrite's *Life* of Saint Nicholas travelled with pilgrims, scholars, merchants and others east to Syria, Palestine and Egypt.

In the East during the tenth century, the widespread popular recognition of Saint Nicholas resulted in a multitude of cultural artifacts. The *Ceremonial Book* of Konstantinos Porphyrogenitos reports the establishment in Constantinople of an asylum bearing the name "Hagios Nikolaos," meaning "Holy Nicholas," within the complex of the Eastern Roman Empire's flagship church of "Hagia Sophia," or "Holy Wisdom." The Holy Nicholas asylum provided shelter and care for the destitute and those afflicted with physical or mental disorders. By the twelfth century, churches dedicated to Saint Nicholas had been established in and around Constantinople, from the Golden Horn to the Galata, across the strait. Saint Nicholas was honoured in the Near East by a church at Bethlehem and by namesakes among the prelates of Antioch and Alexandria. The icon art of the medieval Eastern Roman Empire features Saint Nicholas prominently. Many Saint Nicholas icons of great beauty and antiquity exist today, despite the catastrophic losses suffered by the iconographic legacy during the Iconoclastic Period of the seventh to eighth centuries and the sack of Constantinople in the thirteenth century. With regard to the iconoclast controversy, we learn that the "purists" fought against what they perceived to be the idolatry of icons until after the seventh ecumenical council at Nicaea in 787. From 726, under the Eastern Roman Emperor Leo III, the controversy grew and subsided with the result that many icons were destroyed until the year

843, when Empress Theodora secured the triumph of iconography in the Eastern Orthodox Church. In the year 1204, the Crusaders of the Fourth Crusade unleashed a three-day rampage through the Eastern Roman capital of Constantinople, causing loss of life, injury and the destruction of those icons that had survived the iconoclast controversy. A first-hand commentator, Nicetas Choniates, described the scene as ironically cruel, that men displaying the cross of Christ on their armour and standards should be so merciless and destructive.[93]

Constantinople served as the nexus of trade between East and West, and, just as the popular stories about Saint Nicholas had made their way east with travellers, his fame also followed the trade routes west—first to Italy, and then from Sicily and Calabria—to Western Europe. Evidence of the early spread of his stories is apparent in Rome, where the basilica of Saint Nicholas in Carcere, a church located at a prison, came into existence by the seventh century. In Naples, Johannes Diaconus worked from Greek texts to create a Latin *Vita* of Saint Nicholas in the year 880. His work circulated rapidly in the West and, as a result, Saint Nicholas became hugely popular in Western Europe as the hero of stories, songs, plays and art.

Another avenue for the Saint Nicholas stories to travel opened up in the sixth to seventh centuries, when Irish monks established the learned monastic centres of Iona and Lindisfarne on the islands off the coasts of Scotland and Northumbria respectively. The monks from the Irish church communities of Iona and Lindisfarne, together with their counterparts among the missionary curates of the church at Rome, launched Christian missions to the northern reaches of Western Europe.

Noteworthy among these early missionaries are Columba of Iona, Columbanus of Ulster, Cuthbert and Aidan of Northumbria, Augustine of Canterbury, Wilfrid and Paulinus of York, and Boniface. Differences in church practice between monks of the Irish church centred at Iona and Lindisfarne and curates of the Roman church headquartered at Canterbury caused confusion and were brought before the council at Whitby in the year 664. Bringing the Irish monks and the Roman curates together provided the opportunity for Saint Nicholas stories to reach as far as Northern Europe. The seventh-century missions by monks from the Irish church centres and curates from the Roman church hastened the spread of Christianity throughout England, France, Germany and the Low Countries.[94]

In Germany, during the early ninth century, the prominent Abbot of Fulda and Archbishop of Mainz, Hraban Maur, wrote about the relics of several saints, including Nicholas of Myra. In France, later in the ninth century, Usuard of Saint-Germain-des-Pres popularized the tale of *Three Generals*. Eventually in the sixteenth century, Usuard's summary of *Three Generals* met with the approval of a papal commission under Pope Gregory XIII and was included in the *Roman Martyrology*. This ensured a place of honour for Saint Nicholas of Myra among the saints of the Roman Catholic Church.

During the tenth century, the Church in the West created a liturgical form called the *historia*, in which the celebrants give voice to recitations, songs, lessons and prayers in honour of a saint's day. While the East had already developed special liturgical celebrations for saint days, the first Saint Nicholas historia known in the West appeared in Germany in the tenth century. A noted scholar and musician named Reginold of Eichstätt composed the best-known liturgy in the West to celebrate the feast day of Saint Nicholas of Myra, a distinction that helped Reginold to advance to the bishopric of the diocese of Eichstätt. Reginold probably drew upon Johannes Diaconus' *Vita* to create the Saint Nicholas historia. Once Western Europeans had come to celebrate Saint Nicholas in the popular verses and songs of the eleventh century, their devotion to him grew immeasurably. We include one of the most popular Latin songs of eleventh-century Europe that takes inspiration from Reginold's historia of Saint Nicholas.[95]

Congaudentes exultemus vocali concordia
Let us lift our joyful voices in vocalic harmony
Ad beati Nicolai festive sollemnia.
On the day of blessed Nich'las,
marked with due festivity.
Qui in cunis adhuc iacens servando ieiunia

He, still clinging to his cradle,
practised abstinence by fast,
Ad papillas coepit summa promereri gaudia.
At his mother's breast beginning
to gain merits that would last.
Adulescens amplexatur literarum studia,
As a youth he concentrated on close study of the Word,
Alienus et immunis ab omni lascivia.
Shunning like the plague those bordels
where gross acts of sin occurred.
Felix confessor, cuius fuit dignitatis vox de caelo nuntia,
Exemplar benign, whose worth was of such verity
'twas manifestly God's decree,
Per quam provectus praesulatus sublimitur ad summa fastigia
By which straightway in bishop's robes
by merit he exalted was to high degree.
Erat in eius animo pietas eximia,
Character in him was marked by notable benevolence,
Et oppressis impendebat multa beneficia.
He relieved oppression's victims
with a true munificence.
Auro per eum virginum tollitur infamia,
With the gold, which he expended,
he removed the maidens' shame,
Atque patris earundem levatur inopia.
Indigence alleviated of the father with the same.
Quidam nautae navigantes et contra fluctuum
Certain sailors navigating against a hostile tide,

saevitiam luctantes navi paene dissoluta,
Battling savage counterwinds,
with their vessel might have died,
Iam de vita desperantes in tanto positi
Losing hope of this existence,
in jeopardy constrained,
periculo clamantes voce dicunt omnes una:
Crying out in chorus praying with a fear unfeigned:
"O beate Nicolae nos ad portum maris trahe
"O most blessed Nicholáos,
draw us toward a peaceful haven
de mortis angustia;
From this ghastly threat of hell.
Trahe nos ad portum maris, tu qui tot auxiliaris
Draw us toward a peaceful haven
by thy marv'lous mediation,
pietatis gratia."
Call on God, Who know'st thee well."
Dum clamarent nec incassum, ecce, quidam dicens:
While they clamoured, not unheeded, someone said,
"Assum ad vestra praesidia."
"Lo, here I speeded to your rescue from the deep."
Statim aura datur grata et tempestas fit sedata,
Then the force of wind was lightened,
tempest calmed and heavens brightened,
quieverunt maria.
And the waves reclined in sleep.
Et ipsius tumba manat unctionis copia,

From his tomb there flows an unction
rich in healing cordial
Quae infirmos omnes sanat per eius suffragia.
Which cures ev'ry ill on contact
through his graciousness to all.
Nos, qui sumus in hoc mundo vitiorum in profundo
We who suffer in this world,
in this sin-full vortex whirled
iam passi naufragia
E'en to foundering in the deep,
Gloriose Nicolae, ad salutis portum trahe
Pray to heav'nly Nicholáos to a port of safety draw us,
ubi pax et gloria;
Glorious hav'n of peaceful sleep.
Illam nobis unctionem impetres ad Dominum
Yield to us that healing unction,
granted through the Lord's injunction,
prece pia,
His loving boon—
Qui sanavit laesionem multorum peccaminum
He Who healed the lacerations
of our many divagations
in Maria.
Through Mary's womb.
Huius festum celebrantes gaudeant per saecula
Celebrants, this Feast of Nich'las,
may they all rejoice this day,
Et coronet eos Christus post vitae curricula.

And may Christ grant halos to them
when from life they pass away.

The original stories of Saint Nicholas from Johannes Diaconus' *Vita* were remarkably well preserved, for Reginold's historia of Saint Nicholas remained true to them. And yet, in the popular culture of the next centuries, storytellers often added spurious narratives to the Saint Nicholas tales. One vivid example is the story about three students who suffer at the hands of a homicidal innkeeper—an old and pervasive theme in Western Europe—which somehow appropriated Saint Nicholas as one of its protagonists. The numerous fanciful legends that storytellers attached to the Saint Nicholas tradition after the eleventh century are, however, beyond the scope of this work and our focus is on the original characterization of Saint Nicholas. This, as we have noted, began with the spoken tradition of Myra, Lycia, in the fourth century; Michael the Archimandrite of Constantinople's *Life*, composed during the ninth century, arrived remarkably intact in the West thanks to Johannes Diaconus of Naples, Italy; Usuard of Saint-Germain-des-Pres, France; and Reginold of Eichstätt, Germany; and the legacy was passed into the popular culture of Western Europe in the eleventh century.[96]

During the tenth century, all of Western Europe saw an increase in the creation of Saint Nicholas artifacts. This followed the burgeoning of art and architecture dedicated to Saint Nicholas that had begun in Italy over a century earlier, inspired by Italy's close ties with the Eastern Roman Empire. In Germany, interest in Saint Nicholas intensified in 972 upon the marriage of Otto II to an Eastern Roman princess named Theophano. This royal marriage effectively knitted together the Holy Roman Empire of the West and the Eastern Roman Empire. From the time of their marriage, churches, chapels, cloisters and schools were established in honour of Saint Nicholas. In France during the eleventh century, a similar flourish of construction brought the name of Saint Nicholas to grace churches and abbeys, notably the Abbaye Saint Nicolas in Angers and the church of Saint Nicolas-les-Arras in Artois. In tenth-century England, William the Conqueror established a priory, as part of Battle Abbey in Sussex, in honour of Saint Nicholas.

In 1087, Italian mariners transported the body of Saint Nicholas from Myra to Bari in Italy, in part to rescue him from non-Christian rulers. We are indebted to a cleric of that time, Nicephorus, who wrote the entire story of *The Translation of Saint Nicholas, Confessor*. Nicephorus begins by explaining that Lord Curcorius and other Barian notables had induced him to write an account of the transport of Saint Nicholas' relics. The Barian instigators of the venture were spurred to act quickly upon learning that a group of Venetians were preparing to carry out the same plan. Reaching Myra, the party from Bari sent an armed contingent of 47 mariners to approach the memorial church of Saint Nicholas. The four local caretakers they met at the church were, at first, helpful in showing them the place where the healing liquor of Saint Nicholas flowed. However, when the custodians realized that the foreign pilgrims had come to remove their beloved Ayios Nikolaos himself, they would not co-operate. A Barian sailor drew his sword, threatening to use it unless one of the caretakers revealed the location of the tomb. A wise custodian stepped forward to intervene, challenging the use of threats and force against a servant of God. He also suggested that the source of the holy liquid was probably the saint's body itself, and warned the Barians that Saint Nicholas possessed the power to decide whether they, or anyone else, would successfully move his body. Putting away his sword, the mariner took up a hammer and struck at the marble sarcophagus until it broke open. He then reached inside and removed the relics. Wrapping the body in a silk covering, the jubilant party returned to their ship.

It did not take long for the news to reach the local townspeople, who thronged to the shore. They plunged into the water and pulled at the rails of the ship, wailing for the return of their patron saint. The Barians replied that Myra had enjoyed the benefits of his holy presence for 775 years and now it was time for Saint Nicholas to shine his light upon the world from Bari. As the sun set upon the coast of Myra, the party sailed west, bearing their prize.

The mariners from Bari sailed, with difficulty, along the jagged, rocky coast of Asia Minor as far as Patara, the birthplace of their appropriated saint, while a dangerous north wind arose and threatened to destroy them. They put in at Perdikca in the Aegean Sea, where they sought to discover why their mission should meet with heavenly resistance. They decided to have all the members of the party swear upon the Holy Gospels that they had not stolen anything of the relics of Saint Nicholas. Five of the sailors confessed that they had indeed taken parts of the holy relics. When the culprits restored what they had stolen, the group regained confidence that they might continue on their journey in safety. They arrived in Bari almost one month later, their return voyage having taken from April 11 to May 9 of the year 1087.

Once the triumphant mariners had arrived, the factions in Bari could not agree upon where to place the relics of Saint Nicholas. According to Nicephorus, a dispute erupted between two opposing factions—those who sought to bring the body of Saint Nicholas to the episcopal palace of Lord Urso and those who, with the original party from Bari, sought to place the saint's relics in the domanial court of the monastery of Saint Benedict under the watchful care of Dom Abbot Elias. The dispute led to a violent street clash and the deaths of two adolescents before it was resolved with the two parties agreeing to bring Saint Nicholas to the monastery. The Norman ruler of Bari, Roger Guiscard, entitled Archbishop Urso to build the church for Saint Nicholas, name it in his honour and inter him. On October 1, 1089, the citizens of Bari entombed the relics of Saint Nicholas in their new church. Pope Urban II consecrated the site and Elias, then Archbishop, constructed a hostel to accommodate the flood of pilgrims who came from every corner of Western Europe to worship their beloved Saint Nicholas.[97]

While Saint Nicholas stories inspired expression in popular culture among those who venerated him in Western Europe, he had also become so popular among Russian Orthodox Christians that they made him co-patron of Russia with Saint Andrew and Mary, the Mother of Christ. Mary's Greek title, "Theotokos," means "God-bearer." Russia had been a pagan nation until the year 988, when Prince Vladimir left his royal capital in Kiev and journeyed to Constantinople to be baptized into the Eastern Orthodox Christian faith. When he returned to Kiev from Constantinople, he had married an Eastern Roman princess named Anna and had become the Christian ruler of Russia. Prince Vladimir hastened the spread of Christianity in Russia. Five hundred years later and after the capital moved from Kiev, Moscow inherited the title of "Third Rome," after Constantinople, which had been the "Second Rome."[98]

Among the gifts Prince Vladimir received from the court of Emperor Basil II at Constantinople were the stories of Saint Nicholas and some of his relics, which included icons and phials of holy myrrh. While Christianity began to grow in the hearts of Russians, the stories of Saint Nicholas flourished in their imaginations. Russian pilgrims flocked to the shrine of Saint Nicholas in Bari, which led the Russian government to support a church, hospital and guest house there.

Multitudes of people came to embrace Saint Nicholas as their guardian saint. The earliest groups of people to call upon Saint Nicholas as their patron saint were sailors, children and captives. Sailors claimed the patronage of Saint Nicholas because of the stories of his calming storms at sea and rescuing mariners. Across the Mediterranean Sea, sailors used to wish each other a successful voyage with the saying, "May Saint Nicholas hold the tiller!" We trace his patronage of children all the way back to the story of his donation of money to the destitute parent of three children. He became the protector of captives, innocents, judicial practitioners and even criminals by virtue of the story in which he intervened to save innocents whom a judge had unjustly condemned to execution.

Many other nations, such as Greece, and regions, such as Apulia and Sicily in Italy, Lorraine in France and Fribourg in Switzerland, have come to revere Saint Nicholas as their patron saint. Likewise, numerous cities, such as Bari and Ancona in Italy, and Amiens and Civray in France, look to Saint Nicholas for their protection and blessings. To the north, Saint Nicholas became co-patron of Norway with eleventh-century Saint Olaf Haraldsson. By the close of the fifteenth century, Western Europe had dedicated over 2,550 artifacts to Saint Nicholas of Myra. The Saint Nicholas legacy in Europe has included churches, chapels, cloisters, hospices, altars, cemeteries, paintings, manuscripts and stained-glass windows.[99]

Artists in both the West and East have depicted Saint Nicholas in thousands of devotional works. The first such effort was made in the sixth century, when the Christians of Myra built a small basilica and named it in honour of Saint Nicholas. They placed his remains in a sarcophagus within. The sculptor of the stone coffin shaped a figure of Saint Nicholas in bas-relief on the cover. It is from this sculpture on the sarcophagus that we have our earliest likeness of Saint Nicholas. We see him wearing a hooded, long-sleeved tunic that has a narrow waistband. He has a long, full beard, is a little over five feet tall and has a slight build.

In the icon art of the Eastern Orthodox Church, artists have painted Saint Nicholas according to a traditional set of conventions. We say, "have painted" because they continue to paint him today. Icon painters have depicted his face with white hair and beard. The image of Saint Nicholas that we see in icons wears bishop's vestments—the sticharion is a dress-like undergarment; the epitrachelion is a stole that he wears around his neck and that extends in front almost to the floor; the epigonation is a diamond-shaped emblem hanging from his right hip that represents "the sword of God's truth"; the phelonion is a long, cape-like over-garment; and the omophorion is the specific symbol of the bishop and is a long stole marked with crosses that extend vertically front and back. With his right hand, Saint Nicholas gives a blessing and in his left hand he holds the Gospels, which symbolize his role as a minister of God and teacher of God's truth.

This portrayal of Saint Nicholas constitutes a canon that icon artists in the East have followed from the sixth century through to the present. Let us take a brief tour of a few of the more important icons that have survived to form part of the Saint Nicholas legacy. In the East, we go to Egypt and to the foot of Mount Sinai, where the ancient and still active Monastery of Saint Catherine possesses an unexpected collection of rare Eastern Church icons. A diptych that dates to the seventh or eighth century may be the only icon of Saint Nicholas that predates the iconoclast controversy. This painted wooden panel depicts, in full stature and classical decoration, Saints Paul, Peter, Nicholas and Chrysostom. Another treasure of the Monastery of Saint Catherine is a full-height depiction of Saints Zosimos and Nicholas, an icon in classical style that dates to the early ninth century. Finally, with the eleventh-century icon that came to Saint Catherine's from Syria, the image of Saint Nicholas reaches a style that icon artists have followed ever since. We see the image in classical form of a standing Saint Nicholas painted on a Deesis, which, in the Eastern Church, is a panel at the centre of the icon wall, or iconostasis, dividing the sanctuary from the nave. Now for the first time, we see

Saint Nicholas in the company of the Holy Mother and Christ, which reveals the exalted place to which Eastern Christianity has come to honour him.

Devout Eastern Christians perceive icons as depictions of living persons in settings and moments that transcend space and time—as though one were looking through a window from space-time to a place in eternity—thus the painting of icons is a form of both art and reverence.

Artists in the West began painting images of Saint Nicholas much as their counterparts in the East had done. In the West, we begin our tour of Saint Nicholas art in Italy where, in the eighth century, Greek iconographers had migrated to escape the repression of the iconoclasts in the Eastern Roman Empire. The West's first known image of Saint Nicholas dates to the mid-eighth century and appears with the frescoes in the church of Santa Maria Antigua in Rome. Painted by expatriate Eastern Roman iconographers, one fresco here depicts Christ flanked on his right by Latin Church saints and on his left by their Eastern counterparts, one of whom is Nicholas of Myra. Also at Santa Maria Antigua, we see, in another fresco, the first depiction in the West of a Saint Nicholas legend—although the poor condition of the fresco makes it difficult to know whether we are looking at three destitute children or three imprisoned innocents. What is clear is that the frescoes at Santa Maria Antigua bear the stylistic elements of the Eastern iconographic canon, which the West followed, more or less, for another five centuries.[100]

It is here in Italy, however, where the West begins to paint Saint Nicholas in ways that depart from the Eastern formula. In Italy from the late thirteenth to early fourteenth centuries, the Florentine painter Giotto di Bondone took up the theme of Saint Nicholas' legends and brought them into a new light, into a more temporal and spatial setting illuminated by radiant colour such as one would see in the stained-glass windows of a Gothic cathedral. Giotto's frescoes in the Arena Chapel at Padua, in the Veneto region of Italy, tell the popular stories of Saint Nicholas vividly and with realism. A new emphasis in Western Europe on dynamic storytelling—in the Gothic idiom of light and colour and in three-dimensional space—placed Saint Nicholas in the new and yet, to him, familiar perceptual setting of earthly human experience.[101]

Throughout the medieval period and up to the present, multitudes of people in both the East and West have prayed and still pray to God invoking the intercession of Saint Nicholas. The famous Latin prayer *Innocentium protectio* asks the intervention of Saint Nicholas to protect the wrongly accused.[102]

> God, who graced holy Nicholas as a protector of innocence in danger while he lived, and after his death by infinite miracles, allow that by his virtue we may be spared from injustice while alive and from the fiery pangs of separation from You after death.

The celebrants of an Eastern Orthodox Christian liturgy sing the *Troparion of Saint Nicholas*, a hymn to honour Saint Nicholas.

> Thy work of justice did show thee to thy congregation a rule of faith, the likeness of humility, and a teacher of abstinence, O Father and Bishop Nicholas. Wherefore, by humility thou didst achieve exaltation, and by meekness, richness. Intercede, therefore, with Christ to save our souls.

From the Middle Ages to the present, Western Europeans have imposed dozens of transformations upon Saint Nicholas in the process of fashioning him into Father Christmas. Yet we see evidence of the original Saint Nicholas of Myra in patronages asked of him by his medieval Christian devotees.

To medieval believers in the West and East, Saint Nicholas was the helper to call upon for needs within three areas: spiritual care, justice and material welfare. Setting aside the spurious and wild tales attached to Saint Nicholas after the eleventh century, we can see the direct connection between these patronages and the original stories rooted in the spoken tradition of fourth-century Myra.

The original stories collected by Michael the Archimandrite tell us that, as bishop, Saint Nicholas faced evil and struggled against it with great courage, taking upon himself the ferocious attack against Christians in Myra to protect others during the Great Persecution. He suffered in captivity for years. After his captors released him from prison, Bishop Nicholas rebuilt the community of faithful in Myra and ministered to his parish, nourishing their souls and restoring their lives.

The patronages that our ancestors have asked of Saint Nicholas have established him as a protector of victims of injustice; a guardian of lands and communities; and a provider of spiritual care, justice and material welfare for people in every niche of life. The Saint Nicholas legacy includes churches, schools, hospitals, cemeteries, paintings, manuscripts and stained-glass windows. Bishop Nicholas' most significant gift to the world, however, is that by his Christ-inspired advocacy for the vulnerable, the innocent and the troubled during the early fourth century, millions of people have since come to know the grace, love and protection of God.

Chapter 7

Saint Nicholas in the Christmas Tradition

The Nativity of Christ depicted in the Gospels radiates meaning and mystery. The stories of the Nativity that we read in the books of Matthew and Luke introduce a number of persons, symbols and interactions that we have come to celebrate diversely among the national cultures of the East and West. These nations, possessors of the treasuries of Roman imperial and Christian heritage, have come to celebrate the Nativity with a variety of cultural forms and traditions. Many of our national cultures have given Saint Nicholas a place in Christmas celebrations, in part because his saint day is on December 6, but more importantly because Saint Nicholas offers gifts of his own that have inspired our ancestors to include him with celebrations of the Nativity.

In order for us to understand the various Christmas celebrations begun by our ancestors, we shall revisit the

Nativity in the Gospels of Matthew and Luke, Chapters 1 and 2. An angel delivers the message of the arrival of the forerunner, John the Baptist, who comes in the spirit of Elijah or, in Greek, Elias. The angelic Annunciation to Mary, wherein God calls upon her to deliver Jesus into life on earth, meets with Mary's acceptance. Mary, the Mother of Christ, gives birth to Jesus in Bethlehem in a stable. Joseph provides care and protection to Mary and the infant Jesus. An angel announces the birth of Immanuel who is "God-with-us" to the shepherds; above them, the heavenly host sings Hosanna, meaning "Saviour." The guiding star rises in the East and traverses the sky towards Bethlehem. The Magi follow the star to Bethlehem, where they visit with the Holy Family and attest to Christ's cosmic destiny as the Anointed One, giving him gifts of gold, frankincense and myrrh.[103]

The facets on the gem of the Nativity shined differently in the eyes of beholders among our ancestors from distinct national cultures. We see that the Nativity presents many brilliant aspects and here are but a few: the community of heaven appears in celebratory contact with the community of earth; reconciliation comes from heaven when Mary gives birth to the infant Christ; God's love illuminates the world on a night of celestial mystery; people gather to offer worship and to bring gifts to the Holy Family. The cultural responses that nations with Christian communities have made and how they have come to celebrate Christmas are as varied as the lustrous facets of the Nativity itself.

At the centre of the Nativity are the gifts of love and justice. Love is manifested as God sending Christ into the world and joining heaven and earth in celebration on that starlit night. Justice arrives as God sending Christ to mercifully reconcile people towards divine principles that guide motivation and action.

The gifts of love and justice that we see at the centre of the Nativity form the core qualities in the life of Saint Nicholas of Myra. Love shines through in his service to God as a guardian of souls, as a protector of children and families, and as a provider of gifts. Justice shows forth in his episcopal role as an advocate for the vulnerable, the innocent and the troubled.

Before the Christian era, the Latin pagans of the Western Roman Empire celebrated the feast of Saturnalia from December 17th to 23rd. They honoured Saturn, the god of planting, at the winter solstice. The Greek pagans in the Eastern Roman Empire celebrated the festival of Kronia, dedicated to their god of planting, Kronos. The Roman pagan significance of December 25th changed in the third century, when it came to be celebrated as the "birthday of the sun," from the cult of *Sol Invictus*, which is Latin for the "unconquered sun." This cult grew out of Mithraism, a popular eastern mystery religion.[104]

When the Christians replaced Saturnalia with Christmas, they absorbed both festivals and associated customs into the Feast of the Nativity of Christ. During the Feast of the Nativity, celebrants shared happiness and goodwill, decorated their homes with greenery and candles, and exchanged gifts. Christians transformed the Mithraic image of the unconquered sun into a Christian image of the Nativity of Christ. They applied the scriptural passage from Malachi 4:2 to describe the arrival of the Messiah as the rising of the "sun of righteousness."[105]

Saint Nicholas and other Christians of the fourth century in the Eastern Roman Empire celebrated Christ's Nativity and Baptism on January 6. In the scripture story of Christ's baptism, the Apostle Luke tells us that, after John the Baptist has immersed Jesus in the Jordan River, "the Holy Spirit descended upon him in bodily form, as a dove, and a voice came from heaven, 'Thou art my beloved Son; with thee I am well pleased.'" Fourth-century Eastern Roman Christians celebrated Christ's Nativity and Baptism as a dual Theophany, that is, a two-fold visible manifestation of God. Later, about the year 336, the church at Rome changed the celebration of the Nativity to December 25. The Eastern Church, with exceptions that we will note in more detail, followed suit by 380. The church leaders intentionally changed the date to coincide with, and thus to replace, the celebration of pagan festivals that traditionally occurred around the time of the winter solstice.

A Nativity celebration during the fourth century in an Eastern Roman city, such as Bishop Nicholas' home city of Myra, would have proceeded as follows.

> The celebrants wore festive clothes with colourfully embroidered tunics and they decorated the doors and windows with fresh greenery and candles. They prepared sweets, such as figs, dates and honey, or fashioned handmade gifts, such as decorative candles, clay figures and dolls, or set aside medallions and coins, all of which they gave to their friends and families in imitation of the Magi who bestowed gifts upon Jesus, Mary and Joseph.[106]

Let us now journey around what was once the Eastern Roman Empire—from Greece and the Slavic countries, south to Turkey, then east to Armenian regions, Iraq and Iran, and south to Syria, Jordan, Lebanon, Palestine, Israel, Egypt and Ethiopia—to visit the modern descendants of those Eastern Romans. We will learn about their traditions for the Christmas season, and we will see to what extent, if any, they include a celebration of Saint Nicholas. Afterward, we will set our sights west. Beginning in Italy, we will follow the tradition of Saint Nicholas and the celebration of the Nativity as it developed in what was once the Western Roman Empire.

In modern Greece, Christmas is known by its Eastern Orthodox Church title, the Feast of the Nativity, and is of secondary importance to Easter, which is known as

Pascha. Saint Nicholas has his own feast day on December 6, which the Eastern Christian tradition remembers as the accepted date of his departure from earthly life. This places Saint Nicholas Day well into the Nativity Fast, which runs from November 15 to December 24 on the Eastern Church calendar. During the Nativity Fast, Christians refrain from consuming meat and dairy foods. Saint Nicholas, or Ayios Nikolaos as the Greeks know him, is given a major feast day celebration in Greek Orthodox churches. This calls for a liturgy with special hymns, dedication and communion. The sailors of Greece pay particular regard to their patron saint on the feast day of Saint Nicholas: to those who ply the waters off the rock-bound coasts of Greece, Holy Nicholas of Myra, the rescuer of mariners from disasters at sea, is a most important saint.

As December advances to the Eve of the Nativity, the Greek family prepares large loaves of sweet *christopsomo*, or "Christ's bread," decorating the crusts with festive shapes. One of the loaves has a symbol of the family vocation baked onto the crust. The family sets the table with the loaves of christopsomo, a pot of honey, dried fruits, nuts and other savoury delights. One member of the household makes a sign of the cross over the loaves and greets everyone at the table with *kronia polla*, which, loosely translated, means "Happy Christmas." Then everyone receives a slice of the bread to dip in honey. So begins the Christmas feasting. The Greeks also have a tradition in which they set alight a great log, called a *skarkantzalos*, which burns brightly to frighten away evil spirits, or *Kallikantzaroi*. This ensures domestic peace by providing the bright light of good cheer and keeping away any troublesome influences that might enter the household by way of the chimneys. On Nativity morning, Greek children visit homes in their neighbourhood and sing carols, *kalanda* in Greek, and often receive gifts from the neighbours in the form of dried fruits, nuts and sweets.

The New Year falls on the Eastern Orthodox feast day of Saint Basil the Great, who is known as Ayios Vasilis in Greek. Saint Basil the Great, a late fourth-century monk from Caesarea, in the province of Cappadocia, Asia Minor, came to be much beloved among Eastern Christians for giving sage discourse in theology and providing tender care to the infirm at a church hospital. In honour of Saint Basil, the Greeks bake sweet New Year bread, known as *vasilopita*, in which they hide a coin. One member of the family blesses the bread and then offers the first slice to Christ, the second to his mother, Mary, and the third to Saint Basil. The rest of the vasilopita goes to the family. The lucky person who finds the coin receives a special New Year's blessing from Saint Basil. Family members also exchange gifts on this day. The Greeks came to associate gift giving with the feast day of Saint Basil rather than with that of Saint Nicholas, because Saint Basil's Day coincides with the New Year, when Greeks exchange gifts.

The blessing of the waters by the bishops and priests on Epiphany, January 6, is the occasion for Greek households to fill containers with blessed water. Each family invites the priest into their home, where he uses the holy water to bless the house room by room. In Greek coastal towns, the priest or bishop leads a ceremony at the docks where he blesses the sea and the ships, and then throws a cross into the harbour. Those who are young and fit dive into the water to retrieve the cross, and the person who finds it first has the honour of holding it in a procession through the town.[107]

Let us move north to Russia, where Saint Nicholas is one of three official saintly guardians, together with Saint Andrew and Mary, the Mother of Christ and the Theotokos or God-bearer. Russia chose these saints under the guidance of the hierarchy of the Eastern Orthodox Church in Constantinople, which, for a hundred years, selected the Russian patriarchs. Russia came into close contact with Eastern Christianity in the ninth century, when the missionaries Saint Cyril and Saint Methodius from Constantinople translated the Greek Gospels and liturgical texts into the Slavonic language. In the tenth century, Prince Vladimir travelled to Constantinople to be baptized into the Eastern Orthodox Christian faith. When he returned to Russia, he brought with him the stories and a few relics of Saint Nicholas of Myra, which included iconography and phials of myrrh. As a result, Saint Nicholas stories spread throughout the region and Saint Nicholas became immensely popular in Russia, Ukraine and other Slavic nations.[108]

Russian Orthodox Christians, like their Greek counterparts, celebrate the feast day of Saint Nicholas on December 6. Russians also observe the Nativity Fast, when they abstain from consuming meat, dairy products, vegetable oils and wine. The Russians honour Saint Nicholas Day with a communion liturgy and a feast-day celebration, within the limitations imposed by their fast.

For Russians, Christmas is the Eastern Orthodox celebration of the Feast of the Nativity, and Christmas Eve is part of the Advent season, during which Slavic Eastern Orthodox Christians observe a meatless fast. Even so, Russians celebrate Christmas Eve with a dinner that could include meatless dishes, such as fish, and dairy-free dishes, such as borscht and stuffed cabbage leaves. The primary Christmas treat is *kutya*, a combination of grains and seeds rolled in honey.[109]

Before we travel to our next destination, we must understand that nations in the East celebrate their Nativity and related feasts on different dates from their neighbours in the East and their fellow Christians in the West. People in the Eastern regions, including Greece, Russia and the Slavic nations, celebrate Christmas according to one of two historical calendars. The Julian calendar, named after Julius Caesar, came into being about 45 BCE as the first calendar based on the solar year of 365 days, rather than the lunar year of 304 days. The whole Roman Empire and, later, Western Europe, used the Julian calendar until 1582, when Pope Gregory XIII adjusted the year by 10 days to create the Gregorian calendar, which counts its dates 10 days, more or less, behind the Julian calendar.

The change from the Julian to the Gregorian calendar has held, for some Christians, a theological association, whereby some church leaders have felt that their use of a particular calendar has enabled them to distinguish themselves in principle from other communities, both Christian and non-Christian, who have followed a different calendar system. Be that as it may, many Christians in the Eastern Mediterranean world who prefer to stay with their ancient traditions still use the Julian calendar. The Christians of the East who follow the Julian calendar include those of Russia, Ukraine, Georgia, Serbia and other Slavic states, Poland, the city of Jerusalem and the monastic republic of Simonos Petra, Mount Athos, in Greece.[110]

Ukrainians and other Slavic people who observe the Julian calendar celebrate Christmas on January 6th. The Nativity Fast lasts for 39 days, during which time the faithful avoid meat and dairy products. Just prior to Christmas, households prepare for the Feast of the Nativity by cooking 12 dishes, one in honour of each of the 12 Apostles. The dishes must not contain red meat, so fish is usually substituted, along with borscht, cabbage stuffed with millet or rice, and cooked dried fruit. Dessert consists of *kutya*.

When the feast dishes are ready, the family watches the evening sky, waiting for the first star—the celestial sign that heralds the arrival of Christmas and signals the beginning of the feast. Great excitement, particularly on the part of the children, surrounds the sighting of the star. The family gathers at the table and enjoys the 12-course meal in a spirit of love and awe. Following the meal, the children are given gifts and treats. The family attends midnight liturgy and afterward groups of singers called *kolyadniky* visit homes and entertain families with their songs about the birth of Christ. By tradition, the families offer gifts to the singers.

From Ukraine, we move south to Turkey, which used to be Bishop Nicholas' home on the southwest coast of the Eastern Roman region of Asia Minor. Eastern Orthodox Christians celebrate the Feast Day of Saint Nicholas on December 6, much as their Greek counterparts do. For the Nativity, Christians in Turkey celebrate a three-day festival, during which they visit each other's homes, host dinners, and serve sweetmeats, fruit, yogourt and, of course, Turkish coffee.

Travelling east, we learn that the Armenians retain the ancient observance of Christmas on January 18, a date based in part, on the Julian calendar but with an added turn. The Armenian Orthodox Christians count the date of Nativity almost two weeks behind their Eastern Christian neighbours because, unlike their neighbours, the Armenians did not move their feast date during the late fourth century. We might remember that, in about the year 336, the church at Rome changed the celebration of the Nativity to December 25. The Eastern Church, with the exceptions we have just noted, followed suit by 380.

Armenian Orthodox Christians fast one week before Christmas, eating no meat or dairy foods, and on Christmas Eve they refrain from eating altogether. Armenians attend the communion liturgy at their church on Christmas Eve. Once they have completed their evening devotions, they return home and brighten the house with many lights and begin the feast, usually with a great bowl of savoury rice pilaf. One delicious dish after another appears on the table—shredded chicken breast and wheat seasoned with cinnamon and cooked in olive oil, sweetmeats and cakes—as the family and their guests eat heartily. After the meal, the children go to the single-storey roof of the house and hang handkerchiefs, like sacks, over the eaves. Then they sing and ask for gifts. The adults reach up to fill the children's handkerchiefs with treats, such as dried fruits and sweetened nuts or grains, or with money.

On Christmas Day, everyone's attention returns to the church, because this is the day the priest pours out the sanctified waters. The parish gathers at the church to fill containers with blessed water, which everyone brings home for special blessings and for personal use.

In Iraq, the Eastern Orthodox Christians date back to the days of the first few centuries of Christendom. On Christmas Eve, the family observes a ritual in which all gather in the courtyard of their home and hold lighted candles. A younger child reads the Nativity story from the Gospel. After the reading, an adult lights a bonfire. When the fire burns down to ashes, both adults and children jump over the ashes three times and make a wish. On Christmas morning, when it is still dark outside, the worshippers light a bonfire in the churchyard and carry an image of the Christ Child in procession around the church. The worship concludes with the celebrant reaching and giving the "Touch of Peace" to a member of the parish, who then passes the touch to another. The greeting and touch of the great *salaam* continues until everyone in the parish has received it.

In Iran, traditional home of the Three Magi who, on the first Nativity, followed the star to bring gifts of gold, frankincense and myrrh to the Holy Family, people know Christmas as the "Little Feast," which emphasizes that it is less important than Easter, the "Great Feast." The Christians in Iran observe the Nativity Fast, eating no meat or dairy foods for a month prior to the Feast of the Nativity. They celebrate the Nativity Day liturgy and have communion. After this, they feast together and enjoy each other's company. They do not exchange gifts as part of the Nativity Day, but it is an occasion for the children to receive and to sport new clothes.

Syrian Orthodox Christians begin their festive season on December 4, with the feast day of Saint Barbara, whose generosity towards the poor ensures her a revered place in the Syrian Nativity cycle. The evening before Saint

Barbara Day, each household sets out a table laden with sweetmeats made of nuts, honey and wheat, a grain that symbolizes both remembrance of the dead and resurrection to eternal life. On the feast day, everyone follows the example of Saint Barbara. Parents teach their children about generosity and caring for others, and fortunate families give to the poor and visit the lonely. The evening is a time for music, dancing, singing and having fun.

On December 6, Syrian Orthodox Christians acknowledge the feast day of Saint Nicholas with the celebration of a liturgy for Saint Nicholas, *Thaumaturgus*, which is Greek for "Wonder Worker." On Christmas Eve, some Eastern Orthodox Christians make the pilgrimage from Syria to Bethlehem. In Syria, the Orthodox Christian family locks the outer gates of their homes as a reminder of the years of persecution when worship had to be kept secret. The family gathers in the courtyard, lights candles and stands around a stack of firewood. A younger child reads the Nativity story from the Gospel, then an adult lights the fire. All the family sing psalms as they watch the fire burn. When the fire burns low, they make a wish and jump over the coals.

Before dawn on Christmas morning, everyone goes to the church to attend the Nativity liturgy. Syrian churches build a bonfire of vine stems to honour the Magi with warmth for their cold journey to see the Infant Jesus. The worshippers light the bonfire in the darkness and circle the church carrying an image of the Infant Christ. Children receive gifts on Epiphany, January 6, from the "smallest camel of the Magi," in keeping with the legend of the smallest camel, who had to labour the hardest to make the journey with the Magi to see the Christ Child. When Jesus saw the determination and love of the camel he blessed it with immortality. Every year the smallest camel brings gifts for the children; the story teaches the value of every living creature.

In Lebanon, the Eastern Orthodox Christians celebrate the feast day of Saint Nicholas with a liturgy in the church. Christmas meets with great anticipation in Lebanon, even though it is second in importance to Easter. The Lebanese prepare their households elaborately days in advance, with supplies of sweets, dried fruits, nuts and wine. With all the treats prepared, everyone's thoughts turn to the commemoration of the birth of Christ. From sundown on Christmas Eve, celebrants refrain from eating so that they are prepared for the communion liturgy. The family gathers around an open fire in their courtyards and prays or meditates upon the story of the holy night and of Mary giving birth to Christ. They stand by the fire together all evening, happily anticipating the peals of the church bells that will call them to the midnight liturgy.

At midnight, the bells ring out, echoing across the hills from town to town. Every one of the Orthodox Christians who is able to attend the church celebrates the communion worship. At the reading of the Gospel, a member of the parish brings a baby forward so that the priest may bless the child with the reading. After the liturgy, all wish each other peace—*salaam*—and return home to commence feasting.

The Eastern Orthodox Christians among the Palestinians can celebrate the birth of Christ on January 7 in a midnight liturgy at the Church of the Nativity in Bethlehem. The Church of the Nativity stands over the spot where tradition holds that Mary gave birth to Christ. The Byzantine-style church dates back at least to the reign of the Roman Emperor Justinian in the sixth century, and possibly as far back as Constantine the Great in the fourth century. Beneath the Church of the Nativity, pilgrims descend stone staircases to the cave of the Nativity. On the marble slab that covers the presumed spot of Christ's birth is a 14-point silver star. It is the shared responsibility of the Order of Saint Francis and the order's Greek Orthodox, Armenian Orthodox and Coptic Church colleagues to co-ordinate the celebrations at the Church of the Nativity. Palestinian Eastern Orthodox Christians, along with thousands of other Christian pilgrims from around the world, visit the shrine and kiss the sacred place where they believe Immanuel entered the world two millennia ago.[111]

In Israel, Christians in Jerusalem play host to thousands of pilgrims from East and West who come each year to celebrate Christmas in the Holy Land. Crowds of Eastern Christian pilgrims swarm into Jerusalem to follow devotional processions and pray at holy sites in and around Jerusalem on both January 7 and 19, the dates that follow, respectively, the Julian calendar and the practice of the Armenians.

In Egypt and Ethiopia, where an Eastern Christian tradition dates back to the Apostles in the first century, the Coptic Church celebrates Christmas on January 6. The worshippers gather at church during the night of Christmas Eve. They celebrate the liturgy by forming a colourful and candlelit procession. After they have taken communion and completed the liturgy, they begin feasting and socializing.[112]

Having visited the modern Christian descendants of the ancient Eastern Romans, we see that, as the Nativity approaches, many still commemorate Saint Nicholas, Bishop of Myra. Celebrations often include a feast day and, in the case of some Eastern Orthodox churches, a liturgy with special hymns, dedication and communion.

Let us now journey to the West—stopping first in Italy by virtue of this nation's close ties with the Greek East and because it is the resting place of Saint Nicholas—where we will discover how the modern inheritors of the Western Roman Empire celebrate Christ's Nativity and Baptism and how Christians in the West remember Saint Nicholas of Myra. On their church calendar, the largely Roman Catholic population of Italy has a memorial day of December 6 for Saint Nicholas. Italians in the regions of Sicily, Calabria and Apulia are, by tradition, especially enthusiastic about celebrating Saint Nicholas Day. After all, his relics are entombed at the Basilica di San Nicola in Bari, a city in the district of Apulia.

The traditional celebrations of the Nativity in Italy begin with the novena, nine days of devotion through December 25, and span a three-week period ending with the Feast of the Epiphany on January 6. The Italian faithful observe a strict fast on the last full day before Christmas Eve, the night when each family enjoys a feast. At about 9:00 P.M., the evening mass begins with a solemn and splendid procession of the church celebrants in formal, clerical dress. The Nativity scene, called *presepio* in Italian, at the church can be large and quite artistic. In most Italian homes, handcrafted *presepi* form the centrepieces of Nativity decorations.[113]

We can trace the tradition of the presepio to one person, Saint Francis of Assisi. On Christmas Eve in the year 1223 in Greccio, a sleepy Romanesque town in the Umbrian hills, Saint Francis enlisted the aid of his friend, Giovanni Vellita, to assemble and dramatize the Nativity of Christ in a stable, using real people and animals to depict the events described in Scripture. People flocked to the scene on that starlit winter night where Greccio, like Bethlehem, celebrated a moment beyond time, in the presence of Saint Francis. That celestial Christmas Eve in Greccio enriched for all time two Western European traditions: Nativity plays and manger scenes. Imbued with new meaning and purpose, the presentation of Nativity plays reached a new height of inspiration across Western Europe, while the crafting of exquisite manger scenes reflected a new artistic sensitivity.

As we have seen with other Christian traditions, the person known as the "gift giver" comes in many forms with many stories. So it is in Italy, as well, where on Epiphany, children receive gifts from one of at least two persons—either from *Gesu Bambino* ("Infant Jesus") or from *Befana*, derived from *Epiphania*, a sort of grandmother figure who, legend claims, failed to help the Magi in their search for Christ in Bethlehem and who, in a change of heart, ventured out to bring gifts to all good children.[114]

On the Iberian peninsula, Spain and Portugal approach the *noche buena*, or the "good night," of Christmas Eve with a mixture of gleeful abandon and pious devotion. The brightly lit streets of the cities and towns provide the setting for festive crowds to enjoy the music and colour in the plazas and at the market stalls until the church bells call everyone to midnight mass. The now pious crowds celebrate the *Navidad*, or Nativity of Christ, before joining their families and relatives at home for Christmas dinner. The music, singing and dancing that commenced in the days before the Nativity resume after Christmas dinner. Iberians share with their Italian counterparts a special love for artful manger scenes, called *nacimientos*. On the morning of Epiphany, children receive their gifts from the Magi who, legend has it, passed through Iberia on the eve of Epiphany on their way to Bethlehem.

In Germany, the centuries-old remembrance of Saint Nicholas takes place on December 6. Greenery and decorations go up in the form of four-candle Advent wreaths, holly garlands and Christmas trees. The churches celebrate special services throughout the week leading to the solemn Christmas Eve and Christmas Day observances. The giver of gifts to children, by tradition, is the *Christkind*, meaning Christ Child. Austria, Switzerland and Poland have many Christmas traditions in common with their German neighbours, including the Saint Nicholas tradition on December 6.

The Low Countries and Scandinavia have a Saint Nicholas tradition that dates back to the earliest centuries of trade with the Mediterranean seaports. On December 6, Saint Nicholas arrives in the Netherlands, Denmark, Sweden, Norway and Finland by diverse modes of travel over land or sea. For example, in Amsterdam harbour, Saint Nicholas arrives by way of a ship to great fanfare and pomp.

The Roman Catholic majority of France marks December 6 as a memorial day for Saint Nicholas on their church calendar. France, Belgium and Luxembourg celebrate *Noël*, or Nativity, primarily as a religious and family holiday. The many beautiful churches brighten with extra lamps and, like their sister churches in Italy, construct fine manger scenes, or *crèches*. Children receive their gifts from one of at least two gift givers: *le petit Jésus*, meaning the Infant Jesus, or *le père Noël*, Father Christmas, who derives from Saint Nicholas.

Christmas traditions in the United Kingdom are a blend of ancient and new from home and abroad. While the people of the British Isles approach Christmas as a religious holiday with due solemnity, it is rooted in their nature to celebrate with good cheer. Many churches hold midnight services on Christmas Eve, as well as during Christmas Day. Children receive their gifts from Father Christmas, a modern version of Saint Nicholas. The Christmas tree has been a part of the festival in Britain since Prince Albert and Queen Victoria adopted the tradition from Germany and popularized it in 1841. The Christmas tree that graces Trafalgar Square in London, however, arrives as an annual gift from Norway, in perpetual thanks for Britain's help to the country during World War II.

On their church calendar, the Roman Catholic population of Ireland has a memorial day of December 6 for Saint Nicholas. Ireland celebrates a traditional, continental Christmas. Like France and Italy, Ireland focuses great attention on the religious observance of the Nativity. The churches celebrate special services in the days leading to Christmas Eve, when a midnight Mass takes place, and another Mass commences on Christmas Day. Lovely manger scenes grace the churches and homes across Ireland. Traditional decorations include lighted candles in the windows to offer hospitality to visitors, as well as holly wreaths hung on the doors.[115]

Looking back across the medieval period, we see that missionary saints in the fourth through ninth centuries brought Christian faith in its earliest forms from the church centres of Rome and Constantinople to the furthest reaches of the known world. They brought with them the Gospel stories and church traditions associated with Christ's Nativity and Baptism, which the newly Christianized world celebrated as a dual Theophany. Original stories of Saint Nicholas of Myra followed and, in some cases, accompanied the first Christian missionary saints. The converted Christians in the newly proselytized lands of Latin and Germanic Western Europe and the Slavic nations in the East solidified their responses to both the Nativity and Saint Nicholas stories in ways both original and adopted from neighbours. Such responses found expression in cultural artifacts and celebratory customs that have come to our era as a sumptuous heritage.

As we marvel at this panoply of Nativity and Saint Nicholas culture from our ancestors, we do well to discern, amid its sublime patterns, colours and textures, the original stories that provided the inspiration. The original Gospel stories of Christ's Nativity describe the connection between the divine and the mortal in Immanuel. The Nativity themes of love and justice through merciful reconciliation from heaven towards earth found receptive hearts, even among rulers, in the fourth-century Roman

Empire. When we look back to the fourth century, to the revolutionary point in history when the Roman Empire reoriented towards toleration of Christianity and other religions with Emperor Constantine's Edict of Toleration in 313, we can see the adoption of the cherished and perhaps divine principle of religious tolerance, which contributes appreciably to both the justness and moral success of modern civilization.

The original stories of Saint Nicholas of Myra carry the Nativity themes of love and justice forward in the characterization of a generous and pious servant of God, who guards the souls in his care, protects children and families, and provides gifts for their spiritual and physical welfare, a working bishop who takes dynamic action on behalf of the people as a courageous champion for justice.

Today, millions of people find comfort in their image of Saint Nicholas. He lives as a generous and reassuring presence in their hearts. People represent, celebrate and venerate Saint Nicholas throughout Europe, across the Near East and around the world. The loving devotion and service Saint Nicholas exemplified in his life inspires and reassures many of us now. Far from being a mythical person who we are advised to set aside, Saint Nicholas is a real and heroic person from the tumultuous fourth century, whose victory over evil and generosity of spirit kindles brighter hope in our hearts.

Vita per Michaëlem

Synopsis

In this book we rely upon the stories about Saint Nicholas that Michael the Archimandrite of Constantinople collected into his *Bios* of Saint Nicholas. Michael identified tales that originated with the spoken tradition centred at Myra and assembled them into biographical form. The Archimandrite published his *Bios* of Saint Nicholas of Myra, in Greek, possibly as early as the late eighth century, for we know of its existence in the early ninth century.

Much of what we know about the Greek biographies of Saint Nicholas derives from one authority. The acclaimed scholar Gustav Anrich authored *Hagios Nikolaos, Der Heilige Nikolaos in der Griechischen Kirche; Texte und Untersuchungen* [*Saint Nicholas, The Holy Nicholas in the Greek Church; Text and Notes*] (Leipzig-Berlin, B.G. Teubner, 1913–1917). Anrich presents Michael's *Bios* of Saint Nicholas of

Myra under the Latin title of *Vita Per Michaëlem*. The *Bios*, as Anrich has transcribed it, covers 27 pages, with Anrich's extensive footnotes, and consists of over 600 lines of medieval Greek. Within that text are the original five tales about Saint Nicholas of Myra.[116]

Anrich also presents, in the same cited work, the *Vita Per Metaphrasten* of Symeon Logotheta, or Symeon Metaphrastes, "the Translator." In the stories written by Symeon Metaphrastes we see Saint Nicholas depicted in the narrative style of heroic drama. When we look at how these tales harmonize with the spoken tradition of Myra, however, we see, as other scholars have noted, that there is confusion in the *Vita Per Metaphrasten*, where Nicholas of Sion, a fifth-century Lycian saint, and some of his actions—that he sailed to Jerusalem and calmed a storm at sea on the journey—are mixed in with those of Nicholas of Myra. The evidence supports this argument. For example, Michael the Archimandrite, who wrote one hundred years before Symeon Metaphrastes, does not seem to be confused on these events and does not mention Jerusalem. Since Michael was closer in time to the original Greek spoken tradition, we can have more confidence in what he has told us about Nicholas of Myra.

We can easily reduce the confusion in the narratives of Symeon Metaphrastes by contrasting them with the stories presented in the *Vita Per Michaëlem*. In cases where content in the *Vita Per Metaphrasten* differs significantly from the stories by Michael the Archimandrite, we reduce our valuation of the *Metaphrasten* content's authentic origin in Myra. Where the two authors agree, however, we can combine the content into an original and dynamic whole. By this method we benefit from the best qualities of both authors—we gain both the Myrian origin of Michael the Archimandrite's stories and the narrative drama of Symeon Metaphrastes' tales.

This approach yields five reliable legends about Saint Nicholas, which are woven together by descriptions of the passages in his life. What follows is a descriptive list of the five tales and synopses of each of the five legends. We give the stories here in the order in which they appear in the *Vita Per Michaëlem*, as transcribed by Anrich.

1. *Praxis de tribus filiabus/Praxeon pros tautas treis thiyateras.* Young Nicholas learns that a family is destitute, and the father plans to sell his children into bonded servitude. Nicholas secretly delivers money to the family in order to save them from ruin.
2. *Praxis de innocentes, Praxis de stratelatis/Praxeon pros tous treis stratelatas.* In *Praxis de innocentes,* Saint Nicholas learns that three innocent citizens are about to be executed. He hurries to rescue them, and then confronts the offending magistrate with a charge of injustice due to bribery. In *Praxis de stratelatis,* three innocent generals have been unjustly accused of treason and are sentenced to execution. They pray to God for their rescue, invoking the spirit of Bishop Nicholas of Myra in their prayers. The innocent are released after the

emperor and his praetorian prefect receive visits from Bishop Nicholas, who demands that justice prevail.

3. *Praxis de nautis/Praxeon pros tous nautai*. Mariners at sea become grounded in a severe storm. They pray to God for their rescue, calling upon the spirit of Bishop Nicholas of Myra. The mariners free their ship from imminent destruction and sail to Myra to thank Bishop Nicholas, whom they credit with rescuing them.
4. *Praxis de navibus frumentariis in portu/Praxeon pros ploiou*. A famine has taken hold in Lycia, threatening the whole province, including Myra, with starvation. Bishop Nicholas diverts grain from visiting ships and distributes it to save the people of Myra.
5. *Thauma de Artemide/Thauma pros tes Artemis*. Saint Nicholas warns pilgrims who are en route to visit his church in Myra to dispose of the evil balm they have unwittingly received from Artemis.

We now present synopses of each of the five legends that are based on Michael the Archimandrite's original stories from Myra and reflect Symeon Metaphrastes' heroic narrative style.

1. *Gift to Three Daughters*

Upon the death of his parents, Nicholas considered how to distribute his inheritance to best effect. He had come to know of a man, a widower, in his hometown of Patara who had lost his income and was considering selling his three daughters into slavery. Nicholas was appalled at this possibility and took action to prevent it. He placed an appreciable sum of gold in a cloth sack, crept to the man's house at night and tossed the sack of coins into a window of the house. When the man awakened the next morning, he found the gold, thanked God and provided his eldest daughter with a dowry. A few days later, Nicholas repeated the same act of generosity. When the man found another sum of gold, he praised God out loud and resolved to watch and discover who had rescued him from poverty. After a few days had passed, Nicholas again threw a gift of gold into the house. The man heard the sound and arose to run after his benefactor, calling out for him to stop. He ran fast enough to be able to recognize Nicholas and, reaching him, began to thank him in a great show of affection. Nicholas, however, pulled himself away, insisting that the man promise to keep secret for the rest of his life what had happened.

2. *Protection of the Innocents/Three Generals*

The second legend, and the earliest one to bring fame to Saint Nicholas of Myra, comes in two parts. It begins with the story *Protection of the Innocents*, and concludes with *Three Generals*.

During the reign of Emperor Constantine, there was a rebellion in the Roman province of Phrygia, in Asia Minor. Constantine sent a military force under the command of Nepotianus, Ursus and Eupoleonis. These commanders and their forces set sail for Phrygia, but weather conditions diverted them to Lycia, and they put in at Myra's harbour of Andriaki to wait for a favourable wind. A few soldiers left their ships and went into Myra on an errand to buy food for the rest of the force. Shortly after the soldiers arrived, they argued with merchants and citizens of Myra. This flared into a rampage of looting and destruction in the market district of Myra.

Holy Nicholas, Bishop of Myra, heard the noise and went to the market to quiet the crowds. He asked if anyone had done evil or committed crimes. He then proceeded to Andriaki, where the commanders greeted him and engaged him in conversation. Bishop Nicholas asked the commanders, "From where have you come, who has sent you, and why are you here?"

The commanders replied, "We come in peace. Our benevolent Emperor Constantine sent us to quell a disturbance among the Taiphalis. Unfavourable weather has diverted us here, where we must wait for a fair wind to carry us on our mission."

Bishop Nicholas retorted, "So, the Emperor sent you to quell a disturbance! Why then are you causing a riot in our peaceful city?"

The commanders, who had not been informed about the unruly behaviour of their own soldiers, asked, "Your Holiness, who is causing a riot?"

Nicholas answered, "You are, because you allow your troops to plunder the city marketplace!"

The moment the commanders heard this, they rushed to the market district of Myra. Angered by what they discovered there, they enforced discipline and ordered that the most unruly soldiers suffer physical punishment. They ordered details of soldiers to help the people of Myra repair the damage. Bishop Nicholas invited the commanders to his house for supper.

People ran to Bishop Nicholas from the city of Myra, crying, "Master, had you been present in the city, the magistrate would not have condemned three innocents to execution. We are in despair because we could not find Your Holiness!" Upon hearing this news, Holy Nicholas ran to where a crowd had gathered around the place of execution. The executioner held up his sword, waiting for the Bishop.

When Bishop Nicholas arrived, he found the executioner standing over the three innocents who were bound, kneeling and awaiting their deaths. Immediately, Holy Nicholas boldly snatched the sword from the executioner and threw it to the ground. He released the innocents and took them with him to the city.

Then Bishop Nicholas burst into the chambers of the magistrate, the provincial Prefect Eustathius. The magistrate approached to give him honour, but Nicholas spurned him, saying, "Evil murderer! How do you dare greet me, caught up as you are in so many evil deeds! I will inform Emperor Constantine about your treachery and the manner in which you govern the region he has entrusted to you!"

Hearing this, Eustathius bent to his knees and pleaded to the bishop, "Please do not lay this charge upon me, sir; the truth is I am not guilty, for it was the wish of my masters Eudoxius and Simonides."

Dismissing his plea, Holy Nicholas retorted, "Eudoxius and Simonides did not cause this evil; it was silver and gold." Bishop Nicholas said this because he had learned that the magistrate expected a bribe of a considerable sum to falsely accuse and execute these citizens. Holy Nicholas did pardon the magistrate, after hearing pleas on his behalf from officers of the army and after Eustathius cleared the innocent citizens of his false accusations.

* * *

The three generals, Nepotianus, Ursus and Eupoleonis, received Bishop Nicholas' blessing, then proceeded on their voyage. They successfully carried out their mission to quell the rebellion among the Taiphalis in Phrygia and returned to their emperor, who received them with great celebration.

Some members of the court, however, envied the success and honours enjoyed by these three generals. The rival courtiers came to the Praetorian Prefect Ablabius and said, "The emperor sent the three generals to Phrygia on a mission to quell the Taiphalis, but they plotted with them instead. Then the commanders persuaded their soldiers to join the Taiphalis in a rebellion against the emperor. By this plot, these commanders hope to reign over Phrygia themselves as emperors!" The jealous courtiers paid generous bribes to Ablabius to ensure his complicity in their scheme against the generals.

Ablabius then approached Emperor Constantine and said, "Long life to the emperor! I have been informed that the three generals whom you sent on a mission to quell the rebellion in Phrygia acted outside of your orders. Contrary to your orders, Nepotianus, Ursus and Eupoleonis formed an alliance with the Taiphalis and are planning to attack your Highness. I have arrested them. It is your Highness's decision how to punish them for their treachery, but they should provide an example to deter others."

Upon hearing these accusations, the emperor flew into a rage and ordered the alleged traitors to be executed without trial before dawn. At the prison, the guards received the order of execution from Ablabius and said to the generals, "You will be beheaded soon. If you have any last wishes to share with your families you must tell us quickly."

When the unfortunate three heard from the guards that they were to die, they tore their clothes and lamented, "What did we do against either God or our emperor that we find ourselves condemned? For what offence do we forfeit our lives?"

Nepotianus remembered that upon their recent visit to Myra, Holy Nicholas rescued three innocent citizens from unjust execution. Nepotianus urged his friends, "There is no earthly power that can save us now. Do you remember in Myra, Lycia, how Holy Nicholas saved three innocent men from unjust execution? Could he do the same for us? There is no one other than Holy Nicholas who can rescue us from our fate."

At this, Nepotianus, Ursus and Eupoleonis began to pray to God, invoking the spirit of Holy Nicholas, "Holy One, God of Saint Nicholas who rescued three innocent citizens of Myra from unjust execution, rescue us, Holy One, not turning away from our plight nor forgetting us who are in peril. Rescue us from our tormentors. Please hurry, because we shall be executed before dawn!"

The three condemned generals prayed thus all night. Later that night, Emperor Constantine had a dream in which an imposing apparition demanded, "Emperor, arise now and release three innocent men whom you have unjustly condemned! If you do not obey, God will bring war upon your realm and death to you!" The emperor, greatly confused, asked, "Who are you to make such threats to me, and how did you make entrance into the palace?"

Saint Nicholas replied, "I am Bishop Nicholas of Myra, whom God has sent to demand that you release these three men at once!"

The same night, Saint Nicholas also visited the Praetorian Prefect Ablabius and said, "Ablabius, you who have taken leave of your senses, why have you allowed yourself to accept a bribe, and why have you done such evil to these three innocent men? Free them immediately, or I shall bear witness against your life before God!"

Greatly alarmed, Ablabius asked his accuser, "Who are you and from where do you come, to say such things to me?"

Saint Nicholas replied, "I am Bishop Nicholas of Myra, whom God has sent to command you to immediately release these three men!" Ablabius shuddered at the fearful content of his dream. Just then a palace messenger arrived and announced, "Make haste, the emperor summons you!"

The Prefect Ablabius hurried to the chambers of the emperor, where Constantine described his dream. Ablabius replied that he had had the same dream. Suspicious of the generals, Ablabius advised Constantine that the prisoners should be interrogated about their role in causing the dreams.

Guards brought the condemned men to the palace to be questioned. Emperor Constantine asked them, "By what evil arts have you caused us to have nightmares and insomnia?"

The generals looked blankly at each other, and were unable to grasp what the emperor was asking of them. Fearing that they were being accused of yet another shameful crime, they answered, "Gracious Emperor! We have not cast any spell, nor have we ever said anything against you. We pledge before God that our families raised us to love God and our emperor. We obediently followed your orders to put down the Taiphalis in Phrygia. By the grace of God, we succeeded and looked forward to your favour. Instead, we face dishonour and death."

Emperor Constantine recognized their sincerity, yet he felt unsettled by the night visitation he and his Prefect had experienced. Constantine asked the generals, "Do you know a man named Nicholas?"

Upon hearing this, the generals took heart and told the emperor and his prefect all that they had seen Bishop Nicholas do in Myra, and explained that he had rescued three falsely accused citizens.

Nepotianus described Bishop Nicholas of Myra as a man of such authority that even the Prefect Eustathius would not speak against him. He added, "Great Emperor, because we saw Holy Nicholas rescue the innocent three of Myra, we prayed to God invoking the spirit of Nicholas that we, too, would be cleared of dishonour and false charges."

Emperor Constantine assured the generals that their lives would be spared. He said, "Saint Nicholas has delivered you from death. Prepare yourselves for a journey and put on your uniforms. I send you to give greetings to Bishop Nicholas of Myra and to ask him to pray for the Empire and my reign."

3. *Rescue of the Mariners*

A ship was driven in a gale in a severe storm and ran aground near shore in the eastern Mediterranean. Caught on the shoals, the ship and its company were in grave danger of destruction as wind and waves battered the ship against the rocks. The captain and crew, having heard of Bishop Nicholas as a holy servant of God, prayed to God for rescue by invoking the name of Nicholas of Myra. The sailors claimed to have received help from Bishop Nicholas himself, who appeared to the crew and encouraged them to reinforce the masts and to free the ship from the rocks.

Bishop Nicholas did not limit himself to advancing the prayers of the sailors and giving them encouragement; he gave them strong and expert help. He pitched in to help the mariners strengthen the lines supporting the masts, and he stood with them when they pushed against the rocks with poles to keep their ship from foundering on the shoals in the violent seas. By the intervention of Saint Nicholas, the crew freed the ship, avoided destruction, and resumed sailing along the coast. The moment the ship pulled away from the shoals, Saint Nicholas vanished as quickly as he had appeared.

The sailors steered their ship to the safety of the harbour of Myra, where they went to the church to give prayers of thanks to God for their rescue. They met numerous clerics, but when they saw Bishop Nicholas, they remembered him as Saint Nicholas who had appeared on their ship. Overwhelmed with awe, the mariners bowed to him and asked how he had heard them praying on their ship during the storm. Bishop Nicholas answered that when people devote their lives to seeking the divine, they are able to gain the faculties of clairvoyance in order to see those in danger and clairaudience to hear their cries for help. Bishop Nicholas then advised the mariners to devote their lives to faithful service to God.

4. *Wonder of the Grain Ships in Port*

When famine raged in Lycia, Bishop Nicholas desperately sought grain to feed the starving people of his diocese. Grain ships put into harbour at Myra's sea depot of Andriaki during their voyage from Alexandria, Egypt, to Constantinople, the new capital of the Roman Empire. Bishop Nicholas met with the captains and entreated them to release part of their grain to feed the famine-stricken of Lycia. The captains refused at first, fearing that they would be held to account in Constantinople for any loss of their cargo. Bishop Nicholas persevered, however, assuring the captains that they would not suffer any adverse judgment. He persuaded them to unload hundreds of measures of corn. Bishop Nicholas distributed the grain, which nourished the hungry of Lycia for two years and provided them with seed to plant and harvest.

5. *Wonder of Artemis*

The last of the stories is one of the more curious ones, in that we see Saint Nicholas in conflict with the local pagan deity, known by the Latins as Diana and by the Greeks as Artemis.

> Saint Nicholas, servant of Christ and celebrated Bishop of Myra, had passed from this world to Heaven. During his life on earth, he had performed many wondrous deeds. Even after his death, he continued to inspire others to holiness. Faithful Christians from across the Empire and from every province therein celebrated and revered him. Pilgrims travelled from all regions to pay homage to Saint Nicholas at his church in Myra. One such group of pilgrims prepared to begin their journey to his holy shrine.
>
> While the pilgrims brought their personal goods to the ship in preparation for their journey, they came to the attention of a malevolent spirit who had been driven from the Temple of Artemis by Saint Nicholas and Christians of his community. Just before the pilgrims set sail for Myra, the evil spirit in the guise of a woman approached them. She handed them a jar containing a liquid and said, "Take this jar as an offering to the shrine of Saint Nicholas on my behalf. I am unable to

bring it myself, for I am too ill. When you arrive at the church, I ask that you fill the lamps with this oil."

The pilgrims kindly accepted the jar and set sail for Myra. One night, Saint Nicholas visited one of the pilgrims in a dream and said, "Awaken and throw that jar of evil oil into the sea!" In the morning, the traveller remembered the words of Saint Nicholas and flung the jar into the waves.

Immediately, a flame exploded upon the surface of the sea and in the depths the water boiled violently. The pilgrims were terrified at this catastrophe. The ship lurched and tossed in the violent waves. The crew lost control of the ship and struggled helplessly. The ship's company fell into a desperate panic.

Before all was lost, Holy Nicholas quenched the deadly explosion under the sea. When the danger passed and all fears subsided, the pilgrims and the ship's crew safely reached Myra. Everyone gave joyous prayers of thanks to God for sending Saint Nicholas to their rescue.

NOTES

Introduction

1 Rev. Dr. K.M. George, *The Silent Roots* (Geneva: World Council of Churches (WCC) Publications, 1994), 61. In his penetrating discussion of the hidden and vast sources of Christian life, Dr. George sheds light on the essential qualities of Christian spirituality that define it in relation to other religious traditions. The two qualities of "love and justice" are rooted in the Christian tradition as the core qualities of spirituality. From this, by extension, we derive the core of spiritual authority. We recognize the qualities of "love and justice" demonstrated by Saint Nicholas in the events of his life, and on that basis we affirm his spiritual authority.

2 P. Gerardo Cioffari o.p., *Saint Nicholas, His Life, the Translation of his Relics and his Basilica in Bari*, trans Philip L. Barnes (Bari, Italy: Centro Studi Nicolaini, 1994). In this expert presentation of scholarship and lore about Saint Nicholas of Myra, Father Cioffari reinforces the case for Nicholas as a historical figure with a tradition that contains reliable stories.

3 For example, there is a legend of a poor widower and his three daughters. In Jeanne Ancelet-Hustache *Saint Nicholas* (New York:

Macmillan, 1962), we learn that a widower had fallen upon hard times and was unable to provide a suitable dowry for any of his three daughters. He feared that if he could not support them, he would have to send them out to make their own way in the world when the options for women were regrettably few. Nicholas heard of this and, during three separate nights, he secretly tossed a purse of money into the man's home. On the last evening, the man discovered Nicholas to be his benefactor and thanked him. Nicholas urged the widower not to reveal who it was who had given him the money.

Acceptance of this legend depends upon three criteria. Firstly, is it of ancient Greek origin? Secondly, is it simple and reasonable? Thirdly, do the actions attributed to Nicholas fit with what is known about him and the time and place in which he lived?

To the question of Greek origin, the answer is yes. According to the acclaimed scholarship of Gustav Anrich, author of *Hagios Nikolaos, Der Heilige Nikolaos in der Griechischen Kirche; Texte und Untersuchungen* [Saint Nicholas, The Holy Nicholas in the Greek Church; Text and Notes] (Leipzig-Berlin, Germany: B.G. Teubner, 1913–1917), this legend comes to us from Symeon Metaphrastes, the Greek author of the *Vita per Metaphrasten*, during the tenth century. Metaphrastes' work is probably an elaboration on a previous vita written by Michael the Archimandrite during the ninth century, according to Edward G. Clare, *St. Nicholas: His Legends and Iconography* (Firenze: Leo S. Olschki Editore, 1985). Alban Butler identifies Saint Methodius, Patriarch of Constantinople (d. 847), as the author of the earliest vita, discussed in *Butler's Lives of the Saints*, vol. IV, ed. Herbert Thurston SJ and Donald Attwater (New York: P J. Kenedy & Sons, 1963). The Byzantine hagiographers compiled these accounts of Saint Nicholas from the Greek oral history among Christians of the Eastern Roman Empire.

In adherence to Occam's razor, or the principle that we are to make the fewest possible assumptions in an explanation, let us determine whether this tale contains embellishments. Storytellers in this and other Eastern Roman legends often used a device by which the characters appear in threes: the trios emphasize the Christian Trinity of Father, Son and Holy Spirit. When we reduce the legend's three daughters to two or one, what remains is a specific act of generosity on the part of Nicholas towards a family in need.

Did such action fit with what we know about Nicholas? In *Saint Nicholas: Life and Legend* (Toronto: Fitzhenry & Whiteside, 1975), Martin Ebon cites Symeon Metaphrastes' description of Nicholas as a devoted Christian whose family practised charity and raised him to do the same. In *A History of the Ancient World* (New York: Oxford University Press, 1983) 613-14, Chester G. Starr describes the Diocletian-era Christian Churches and their clergy as providing for the social welfare in their cities with a zeal unknown among the imperial institutions or prominent citizens. These communities of faithful and their leaders provided for the poor, the infirm, widows and orphans. So, we can accept, with reduction, the tale of Nicholas' charity towards a family in need because it is of ancient Greek origin, is simple and reasonable, and is consistent with what we know about Nicholas and the setting in which he lived.

Another legend comes to us from Symeon Metaphrastes, by way of Anrich and Ancelet-Hustache. In this account, three Roman commanders were sent with their armies to quell a rebellion in Phrygia. While they were encamped at Myra, the troops harassed the residents of the city. Nicholas complained to the commanders, who then restrained their soldiers.

Greek tradition tells of Nicholas intervening to save victims of false prosecution. Bishops received from Emperor Constantine the authority in their cities and towns to hear law cases and render judgment that could not be appealed. In Myra, the relatives and friends of victims of injustice certainly would have sought the help of Bishop Nicholas and would have appealed to him for final judicial remedy.

In one incident described in the Greek tradition, residents of Myra called upon Bishop Nicholas, who was still accompanied by the visiting Roman commanders, to intercede on behalf of three innocents who had been wrongly accused and sentenced to death. The residents claimed that the magistrate rendered judgment after receiving a bribe. Nicholas rushed to the place where the innocents awaited execution. He commanded the executioner to stop, released the innocents and confronted the magistrate with a charge of bribery, to which he confessed.

There is an extension to this legend—of Bishop Nicholas saving three innocents from the corrupt magistrate—that describes three Roman commanders returning to Constantinople where they too became the victims of false prosecution at the hands of the Prefect Ablabius. He accused them before the Emperor Constantine and imprisoned them to await execution. The extended account relates that they appealed to the God of Saint Nicholas, who intervened by sending Nicholas' spirit into the dreams of the emperor and his prefect. Nicholas admonished them to let these innocent men go free.

According to the textual analysis, we find that this story is of ancient Greek origin, that it employs three major characters whom we could reduce to one or two Roman commanders and maligned townspeople, that it agrees with what Symeon Metaphrastes reported about Nicholas' passion for justice, and is historically consistent with the nature of a bishop's role in the late Roman Empire. As for the extension to the story, there were two imperial generals in Constantine's service: Flavius Nepotianus, who was consul in the year 336, and Flavius Ursus, who was consul in 338. The Praetorian Prefect Ablabius was a real functionary in the reign of Constantine. So, with Constantine and Nicholas, we have historical support for five of the six characters in the story. Yet, since the story relates that Saint

Nicholas appeared in the dreams of Constantine and his Prefect Ablabius, the supernatural details of the story fall outside the scope of this work (see Clare, *Saint Nicholas*, 14).

Five legends of Nicholas, which originate with the spoken tradition centred at Myra, come to us from the Greek tradition, notably from Michael the Archimandrite by way of Anrich and Clare. These are *Praxis de tribus filiabus*, *Praxis de innocentes*, *Praxis de nautis*, *Praxis de navibus frumentariis in portu* and *Thauma de Artemide*.

4 Charles W. Jones, *Saint Nicholas of Myra, Bari, and Manhattan* (Chicago: University of Chicago Press, 1978), chaps. 1 and 2. Question: How can we be confident that Saint Nicholas of Myra is real? In his thorough and detailed analysis of the legends about Saint Nicholas, Charles W. Jones points out that Myra, by its important role in merchant shipping in the Eastern Roman Empire of the fourth century, was an appropriate site for developing a cult. Bishop Nicholas' eventful life there brought fame to his diocese of Lycia. History supports Bishop Nicholas as the person at the source of the Saint Nicholas cult that emerged during the reign of Emperor Constantine I.

Chapter 1

5 Charles Deihl, *Byzantium: Greatness and Decline*, transl. Naomi Walford, (New Brunswick, NJ: Rutgers University Press, 1957), 112.

6 Cyril Mango, *Byzantium: The Empire of New Rome* (New York: Charles Scribner's Sons, 1980), 61-62.

7 Cyril Mango, *Byzantium*, 61-62. The temple of Artemis in Ephesus, one of the seven wonders of the ancient world, was destroyed by the Goths in 262.

8 Lesley Adkins and Roy A. Adkins, *Handbook to Life in Ancient Rome* (New York: Oxford University Press, 1994), chap. 9.

9 Henry Chadwick, *The Early Church* (Baltimore, MD: Penguin Books, 1967), 278-79.

10 Hieromonk Makarios of Simonos Petra [Mount Athos, Greece], *The Synaxarion: The Lives of the Saints of the Orthodox Church*, vol. 2, transl. Christopher Hookway, (Ormylia [Chalkidike], Greece: Holy Convent of the Annunciation of Our Lady, Distribution, 1999), 333, and Ebon, *Saint Nicholas*, 10.

11 Andrew Louth and Maxwell Staniforth, eds. and trans., *Early Christian Writings* (London: Penguin, 1987), 191-98.

12 Adkins and Adkins, *Handbook*, chap. 9.

13 Chadwick, *The Early Church*, 272.

14 Adkins and Adkins, *Handbook*, 260.

15 A.H.M. Jones. *The Decline of the Ancient World* (London: Longmans, Green and Co., 1966), chap. 3.

16 Paul Veyne et al., *A History of Private Life, From Pagan Rome to Byzantium*, transl. Arthur Goldhammer, (Cambridge, MA: Belknap Press, Harvard University Press, 1987), 117-37.

Chapter 2

17 Charles W. Jones, *Saint Nicholas*, 52-53.

18 K.M. George, *The Silent Roots*, 61.

19 Marjorie Colvile Strachey, *The Fathers Without Theology* (New York: George Braziller, 1958), 201-202.

20 Adkins and Adkins, *Handbook*, 188-89.

21 Louth and Staniforth, *Early Christian Writings*, 191-98.

22 Louth and Staniforth, *Early Christian Writings*, 23-50.

23 Louth and Staniforth, *Early Christian Writings*, 119-24.

24 *The New Oxford Annotated Bible, With Apocrypha*, RSV, eds. Herbert G. May and Bruce M. Metzger (New York: Oxford University Press, 1962), Acts 4:32-35.

25 Charles W. Jones, *Saint Nicholas*, 54-57.

[26] This description of Caesarea comes to us from Josephus in William Whiston's translation of *Wars of the Jews*, bk. I, chap. XXI, in *Josephus: Complete Works*,(Grand Rapids, MI: Kregel Publications, 1976), 453. Over the question of which Nicholas travelled to the Holy Land—Nicholas of Myra or Nicholas of Sion—there has been some scholarly scrapping. Some historians think Nicholas of Sion, who lived a hundred years after Nicholas of Myra, was the one who travelled to Jerusalem. They think this is the case because they see some confusion in the stories of Symeon Metaphrastes, where Nicholas of Sion and some of his activities—that he sailed to Jerusalem and calmed a storm at sea on the journey—are mixed in with those of Nicholas of Myra. The evidence appears to be strongly in support of their argument. For one thing, Michael the Archimandrite, who wrote a hundred years before Symeon Metaphrastes, does not seem to be confused on these events and does not mention Jerusalem. Since Michael the Archimandrite was closer in time to the original Greek spoken tradition we may have more confidence in what he had to say about Nicholas of Myra. For more discussion about this question, see Cioffari, *Saint Nicholas*. Symeon Metaphrastes' mistakenly attributing Nicholas of Sion's travels and deeds to Nicholas of Myra does not exclude the possibility that Nicholas of Myra may also have journeyed to the Holy Land.

[27] *New Oxford Annotated Bible*, Acts 27:13-20.

[28] *New Oxford Annotated Bible*, John 15:1-8, and Louth and Staniforth, *Early Christian Writings*, 191-98.

[29] Chadwick, *The Early Church*, 279.

[30] Veyne et al., *History of Private Life*, 270.

[31] Chadwick, *The Early Church*, 274-75.

[32] Mango, *Byzantium*, 228.

[33] Adkins and Adkins, *Handbook*, 341.

[34] Eusebius [of Caesarea], *The History of the Church*, ed. Andrew Louth, transl. G.A. Williamson (London: Penguin, 1989), 2.17, 50-54.

[35] Lactantius [of Bithynia], *The Divine Institutes*, transl. Sister Mary Francis McDonald, o.p. (Washington, DC: Catholic University of America Press, 1964), bks. I-VII.
[36] Lactantius [of Bithynia], *The Divine Institutes*, bks. I-VII.

Chapter 3

[37] Hieromonk Makarios, *The Synaxarion*, 333.
[38] Edward Gibbon, Esq., *The Decline and Fall of the Roman Empire*, vol. I (New York: The Co-Operative Publication Society, n. d.), 654.
[39] Charles W. Jones, *Saint Nicholas*, 58-60.
[40] Eusebius, *History of the Church*, bk. 7.
[41] Gibbon, *Decline and Fall*, 651-53.
[42] A.H.M. Jones, *Decline of the Ancient World*, 30.
[43] A.H.M. Jones, *Constantine and the Conversion of Europe* (Toronto: University of Toronto Press, 1978), chap. 1.
[44] A.H.M. Jones, *Constantine and the Conversion of Europe*, chap. 1.
[45] Hieromonk Makarios, *The Synaxarion*, 333.
[46] A.H.M. Jones, *Constantine*, chap. 4.
[47] A.H.M. Jones, *Constantine*, chap. 4.

Chapter 4

[48] Eusebius, *History of the Church*, bk. 8.
[49] Lactantius, *The Deaths of the Persecutors*, transl. Sister Mary Francis McDonald, o.p. (Washington, DC: Catholic University of America Press, 1965), chap. 16.
[50] Eusebius, *History of the Church*, bk. 8.
[51] A.H.M. Jones, *Constantine*, chap. 4.
[52] Eusebius, *History of the Church*, bk. 8.
[53] Gibbon, *Decline and Fall*, 655-57.

[54] Lactantius, *The Divine Institutes*, bk. 5.
[55] Eusebius, *The History of the Church*, bk. 8.
[56] *Pen and ink graphic rendering of Letter from Arycanda, Lycia, dated about CE 312* (Ottawa, Canada: 2002). The original letter is housed in the Museum of Istanbul (formerly Constantinople), Turkey.
[57] Eusebius, *History of the Church*, bk. 8.
[58] Eusebius, *History of the Church*, bk. 8.
[59] Ammianus Marcellinus, *The Later Roman Empire*, eds. Walter Hamilton and Andrew Wallace-Hadrill (London: Penguin, 1986), bk. 14, chap. 6, 45-50.
[60] Lactantius, *Deaths of the Persecutors*, chap. 18.
[61] Lactantius, *Deaths of the Persecutors*, chap. 23.
[62] Eusebius, *History of the Church*, bk. 8.
[63] Lactantius, *Deaths of the Persecutors*, chap. 32.
[64] Eusebius, *History of the Church*, bk. 9.
[65] Eusebius, *History of the Church*, bk. 9.
[66] A.H.M. Jones, *Decline of the Ancient World*, 323-24.
[67] Adkins and Adkins, *Handbook*, 290-91.
[68] Veyne et al., *History of Private Life*, 262.
[69] Louth and Staniforth, *Early Christian Writings*, 109-11.
[70] Lactantius, *Deaths of the Persecutors*, chap. 49.
[71] Gibbon, *Decline and Fall*, 679. Gibbon made a credible estimate of the minimum Christian losses suffered during the Great Persecution. He began with primary source evidence for 94 executions of Christians in Palestine between 303 and 313, then he applied that number as a possible count for the other fifteen provinces of the East. Using Gibbon's method, we may conservatively guess that at least 1,500 Christians could have suffered death at the hands of Diocletian, Galerius and Maximinus Daia. When we add to that number those who suffered under Maximian in the West, we come to about 2,000 red martyrs for Christ. Yet we should remember that 2,000 is an estimated *minimum* total of martyrs based on scarce historical literature and conservative numbers. The actual losses were probably higher than 2,000.

Chapter 5

[72] Eusebius, *History of the Church*, bk. 10.
[73] A.H.M. Jones, *Constantine*, 93-94.
[74] A.H.M. Jones, *Constantine*, 98-100.
[75] A.H.M. Jones, *Constantine*, 112-15.
[76] Charles W. Jones, *Saint Nicholas*, 27-28.
[77] A.H.M. Jones, *Constantine*, 55.
[78] Strachey, *Fathers Without Theology*, 203.
[79] Eusebius, *The Life of Constantine*, bk. II, Intro., transl. and commentary Averil Cameron and Stuart G. Hall (Oxford: Clarendon Press, 1999), 116-19.
[80] Eusebius, *Life of Constantine*, bk. III, 123-25.
[81] A.H.M. Jones, *Decline of the Ancient World*, 43-44.
[82] Eusebius, *Life of Constantine*, bk. III, 127.
[83] Cioffari, o.p., *Saint Nicholas*, 13. In the *Historia Tripartita*, dated 510 and attributed to Theodore the Lector, the name of "Nikolaos" appears on the tenth line of text among the names of those who attended the Council of Nicaea. See also, Butler, *Lives of the Saints*, vol. IV, 504. Saint Methodius reported that Bishop Nicholas prevented the Arian teachings from taking hold in Myra, but makes no mention of his having attended the Council. Symeon Metaphrastes by contrast reported that Bishop Nicholas not only attended the Council, but got so angry at Arius that he struck him.
[84] A.H.M. Jones, *Decline of the Ancient World*, 46.
[85] Charles W. Jones, *Saint Nicholas*, 29-32.
[86] A.H.M. Jones, *Decline of the Ancient World*, 47.
[87] Steven Runciman, *The Byzantine Theocracy* (Cambridge: Cambridge University Press, 1977), 22.
[88] Eusebius, *Life of Constantine*, bk. III, 140.

Chapter 6

[89] Martin Ebon, *Saint Nicholas: Life and Legend* (Toronto: Fitzhenry & Whiteside, 1975), 40-41.

[90] Charles W. Jones, *Saint Nicholas,* 30-32.

[91] Ammianus Marcellinus, *The Later Roman Empire*, eds. Walter Hamilton and Andrew Wallace-Hadrill (London: Penguin, 1986), bk. 15, chap. 13, 86-87.

[92] Anrich, *Hagios Nikolaos,* vol. I, 118-39.

[93] Ebon, *Saint Nicholas,* 14-15; Gerardo Cioffari, *Saint Nicholas,* Intro.; Clare, *Saint Nicholas*, 15-22; Timothy Ware (Bishop Kallistos of Diokleia), *The Orthodox Church* (London: Penguin, 1993), chaps. 4 and 6. With an eminently fair and scholarly tack, Ware (Kallistos) describes two catastrophes in Constantinople—the Iconoclast controversy and the sack of the city.

[94] George Holmes, ed., *The Oxford History of Medieval Europe* (Oxford: Oxford University Press, 2001), chap. 1.

[95] Charles W. Jones, *Saint Nicholas,* 93-123. Reginold of Eichstätt composed the best-known liturgy in the West to celebrate the feast day of Saint Nicholas of Myra.

[96] Charles W. Jones, *Saint Nicholas,* 176-193.

[97] Charles W. Jones, *Saint Nicholas,* 176-193.

[98] Ware, *Orthodox Church*, chaps. 4 and 6.

[99] George McKnight, *St. Nicholas, His Legend and His Role in the Christmas Celebration and Other Popular Customs* (Williamstown, MA: Corner House, 1974), chap. VIII and Clare, *Saint Nicholas,* 103-15.

[100] Edward G. Clare, *Saint Nicholas,* 51-101.

[101] Edward G. Clare, *Saint Nicholas,* 51-101.

[102] Charles W. Jones, *Saint Nicholas,* 41.

Chapter 7

[103] *New Oxford Annotated Bible*, Luke 2:21-23, and Dmitri Tselos, "The Enigma of Saint Basil, Santa Claus in Modern Greece," *The Greek Star* (Chicago: Thursday, December 22, 1988). Question: Did Christians of the fourth century celebrate the Feast of the Nativity? Yes, they celebrated Christ's Nativity and Baptism on January 6 as a dual Theophany, until the Church at Rome changed the celebration of Nativity to December 25 at about 336, and the Eastern Church followed suit by 380.

[104] Adkins and Adkins, *Handbook*, 287.

[105] Erwin Panofsky, *Meaning in the Visual Arts* (New York: Doubleday, Phoenix edition 1982), 257-60.

[106] Tselos, "Enigma of Saint Basil."

[107] Maria Robbins and Jim Charleton, *A Christmas Companion* (Toronto: Perigee Books, 1989).

[108] Ware, *Orthodox Church*, chaps. 4 and 6.

[109] Herbert H. Wernecke, *Christmas Customs Around the World* (Philadelphia: Westminster Press, 1959).

[110] Ware, *Orthodox Church*, 301-303, and Adkins and Adkins, *Handbook*, 337.

[111] William Sansom, *A Book of Christmas* (Toronto: McGraw-Hill, 1968), 86-87.

[112] Wernecke, *Christmas Customs*, 54-55.

[113] Sansom, *Book of Christmas*, 106, 126-27.

[114] Sansom, *Book of Christmas*, 105-107.

[115] Wernecke, *Christmas Customs*, 50.

Vita

[116] Gustav Anrich, *Hagios Nikolaos*, 113-39, 235-67.

Index

A

B

C

F

G

H

I

N

O

P

R

S